Sunset
Cooking for Two
...or Just for You

By the Editors of
Sunset Books and
Sunset Magazine

Lane Publishing Co. • **Menlo Park, California**

Great Recipes Tailored to Size

Whatever your reason for dining à *deux*, here's a book full of special dishes cut down to size for you and your companion.

Everything is easier when you are two...grocery shopping, food preparation, cleanup. With only two schedules to be considered, your eating hours can be as flexible as you both like; so can the place you choose to dine, for it's not much of a balancing trick to carry two plates to the fireside, TV room, or patio.

With this book, you can tell at a glance how much time each recipe will take. A little clock symbol ⏱ identifies this information, which appears under each recipe title.

We've tailored our soup, salad, sandwich, and egg/cheese chapters for the working couple all too familiar with the effect that business lunches can have on dinner appetites. The meat, poultry, and seafood chapters offer heartier entrées still with no leftovers to deal with.

For-one cooks will also find the book useful, since a number of recipes appear in for-one quantities, while virtually all the others—even if made in for-two proportions—will yield leftovers to please, not to inundate. Each recipe makes two servings unless otherwise indicated.

We wish to extend thanks to Diane L. Dyson for her special assistance in the preparation of this book.

Supervising Editor: Judith A. Gaulke
Research and Text: Cynthia Scheer

Special Consultant: Joan Griffiths
Design: Cynthia Hanson
Photography: Nikolay Zurek
Photo Editor: Lynne B. Morrall
Illustrations: Mary Knowles

Cover: Rack of Lamb for Two (page 41). Each diner gets four ribs. Accompany with Curried Egg and Shrimp-stuffed Tomatoes (page 15) and broccoli spears. Photographed by Nikolay Zurek.

Editor, Sunset Books: David E. Clark

Third Printing January 1980

CONTENTS

SOUPS

Great soup once meant enormous pots of fragrant ingredients that required hours of simmering and resulted in days of leftovers for all but the largest of families. Then there was okay soup, the kind you got by opening a can and adding some milk or water.

This chapter brings you the best of both—recipes for soups that are great, in quantities just right for two (or for one, with one handy serving left to enjoy another day), and with much of the convenience and speed of canned soups. Indeed, many start with canned broth and go on to such special touches as vegetables that still have crunch, bits of crisp bacon, chunks of tender seafood or spicy sausage, spinach-laden meatballs, dollops of cool sour cream. Some can be made ahead, served chilled or reheated to be enjoyed later.

Soup is perfectly portable —when you're in a mood to sit by the fire or on the patio and exchange events of the day, or to relax and let TV bring you up to date on events in the world, a mug of steaming soup is convenient and satisfying.

These recipes begin with light soups, the kind that round out a sandwich or salad meal. Next come the hearty soups that are a meal on their own, well able to satisfy the most enthusiastic appetite with nothing more than some good bread alongside.

Creamy Mushroom Soup

🕐 *Preparation time (cooking included): 10 minutes*

A rich-tasting soup without the calories, this one whips up in minutes. Sip it from a mug, accompanied by a salad or sandwich.

- 1½ tablespoons butter or margarine
- ¼ pound mushrooms, coarsely chopped
- 1 small onion, coarsely chopped
- 1 tablespoon all-purpose flour
- 2 cups milk
- 1 chicken bouillon cube
- ⅛ teaspoon thyme leaves
  - Salt and pepper

In a wide frying pan, melt butter over medium heat. Add mushrooms and onion; cook, stirring, until onion is limp and juices evaporate. Stir in flour and cook until bubbly; remove from heat. Gradually stir in milk. Add bouillon cube (breaking up with spoon) and thyme leaves. Cook, stirring constantly, until thickened.

Whirl soup in a blender or food processor until smooth. Add salt and pepper to taste.

Curried Broccoli Soup

🕐 *Preparation time (cooking included): 10 minutes*

Cool, green broccoli purée comes alive with a nip of curry. Garnish servings with chopped salted peanuts. It's good hot or cold. (See photograph on page 34.)

- 1½ tablespoons butter or margarine
- 1 small onion, chopped
- ¾ teaspoon curry powder
- 1 can (about 14 oz.) regular-strength chicken broth
- 1 package (10 oz.) frozen chopped broccoli, thawed
  - Sour cream
  - Chopped salted peanuts

In a 3-quart pan, melt butter over medium heat; add onion and curry powder and cook until onion is limp. Stir in broth and broccoli and cook, covered, until broccoli is heated through and fork tender (about 3 minutes).

Whirl soup, a portion at a time, in a blender or food processor until smooth. Serve hot or cold; reheat if made ahead. Top with a dollop of sour cream and a sprinkling of chopped peanuts.

Quick Gazpacho

⏱ *Preparation time: 10 minutes. Chilling time: 30 minutes*

Served icy cold, this chunky gazpacho is quick to put together and can be made a day ahead. (See photograph on page 18.)

⅓ cup chopped cucumber
¼ cup finely chopped mild red or white onion
1 small avocado, peeled, pitted, and diced
¼ teaspoon oregano leaves, crumbled
1½ tablespoons olive oil or salad oil
1 tablespoon wine vinegar
2 cups tomato juice
Salt and pepper
Ice cubes (optional)
Lime wedges

In a serving bowl or pitcher, combine cucumber, onion, avocado, oregano, oil, and vinegar. Pour in tomato juice. Cover and chill thoroughly. Add salt and pepper to taste. Add ice cubes to individual servings, if you wish. Pass lime wedges to squeeze over.

Pacific Halibut Soup

⏱ *Preparation time: 10 minutes. Cooking time: 30 minutes*

You add the fish to this soup at the very last minute, and it stays moist and flaky in the seasoned tomato broth with rice and green beans. With warm garlic-buttered French bread, it makes a perfect supper.

1 tablespoon olive oil or salad oil
1 medium-size onion, chopped
1 small clove garlic, minced or pressed
⅓ cup thinly sliced celery
1 can (1 lb.) tomatoes
1 can (about 14 oz.) regular-strength chicken broth
½ teaspoon Italian herb seasoning or ¼ teaspoon *each* oregano leaves and dry basil
2 tablespoons rice
1 cup frozen cut green beans, thawed
½ to ¾ pound halibut, thawed if frozen
Salt and pepper
Chopped parsley
Grated Parmesan cheese (optional)

Heat oil in a heavy 4-quart pan over medium heat; add onion, garlic, and celery. Cook, stirring, until onion is limp. Stir in tomatoes (break up with a spoon) and their liquid, broth, Italian herbs, and rice. Cover and simmer for 15 minutes. Add beans and simmer, covered, for about 10 minutes longer or until rice and beans are tender to bite.

Meanwhile, remove skin and bones from fish and cut into about 1-inch pieces. Add to soup and simmer just until fish flakes readily when prodded with a fork (about 5 minutes). Season with salt and pepper to taste. Sprinkle individual servings with parsley and pass Parmesan cheese to spoon over each serving, if you wish.

Sherry Clam Chowder

⏱ *Preparation time (cooking included): 15 minutes*

Sprinkle crisp bacon over chowder at the last minute and garnish with spoonfuls of sour cream.

4 slices bacon, cut in small pieces
1 medium-size onion, finely chopped
½ cup finely chopped celery
1 can (about 11 oz.) condensed cream of potato soup
1 bottle (8 oz.) clam juice
½ cup milk or half-and-half (light cream)
1 can (7 oz.) minced clams
1 tablespoon dry sherry
Salt and pepper
Sour cream

In a 3-quart pan over medium heat, cook bacon until crisp; set aside. Discard all but 2 tablespoons of the drippings. Add onion and celery and cook until limp, stirring occasionally. Add potato soup, clam juice, milk, and minced clams and their liquid; heat through, stirring. Stir in sherry, add salt and pepper to taste, and sprinkle over reserved bacon. Top with spoonfuls of sour cream.

Lazy Cioppino

Preparation time (cooking included): 10 minutes

No cracking of shells or cleaning of shrimp here. Just buy crab and shrimp meat at the fish market, open a few cans, heat, and you have cioppino!

2 tablespoons butter or olive oil
1 small onion, finely chopped
1 clove garlic, minced or pressed
¼ teaspoon *each* oregano leaves and crumbled
    bay leaves
    Dash sage
1 can (14 oz.) pear-shaped tomatoes
1 tablespoon tomato-based chili sauce
1 can (8 oz.) tomato sauce
¼ pound *each* crab meat and small cooked shrimp
    Water (optional)
    Salt and pepper

Melt butter in a 2-quart pan and cook onion and garlic over medium heat until limp. Stir in oregano, bay, sage, tomatoes (break up with a spoon) and their liquid, chili sauce, tomato sauce, crab, and shrimp; heat through. Add water for thinner soup, if you wish, and salt and pepper to taste.

Cabbage and Ham Soup

Preparation time (cooking included): 15 minutes

Chunks of ham, purchased from a deli or left over from baked ham, are added to sautéed cabbage in a light broth. Top with dollops of sour cream.

3 tablespoons butter or margarine
2 tablespoons finely chopped celery
¼ cup finely chopped onion
1 tablespoon chopped parsley
1 tablespoon all-purpose flour
1 can (about 14 oz.) regular-strength chicken
    broth
½ pound cooked ham, diced
½ teaspoon crumbled bay leaf
1 cup finely shredded cabbage
    Sour cream

Melt 2 tablespoons of the butter in a 2-quart pan over medium heat; add celery, onion, and parsley and cook until limp. Stir in flour. Add broth and cook, stirring, until bubbly. Add ham, bay leaf, cabbage, and remaining 1 tablespoon butter; cook until ham is heated through and cabbage is limp.

Spoon sour cream into individual portions.

Vegetable-Cheese Soup

Preparation time: 15 minutes. Cooking time: 15 minutes

Instant mashed potatoes and canned chicken broth speed the making of this vegetable soup. Stir in cheese chunks just before serving.

2 tablespoons butter or margarine
1 medium-size onion, minced
2 large carrots, cut into thin diagonal slices
1 stalk celery, cut into thin diagonal slices
1 can (about 14 oz.) regular-strength chicken
    broth
    Instant mashed potatoes (amount for 2
    servings), prepared according to package
    directions
½ cup milk
¼ teaspoon *each* seasoned salt and celery seed
    Dash pepper
    About 3 ounces jack or Cheddar cheese, diced
    Ground mace (optional)

Melt butter in a 3-quart pan over medium heat; add onion and cook until limp. Add carrots, celery, and chicken broth. Cover and cook over low heat until vegetables are fork tender (about 10 minutes). Remove from heat and stir in prepared instant mashed potatoes. Add milk, seasoned salt, celery seed, and pepper.

Return to heat until hot through—do not boil. Remove from heat, add cheese, cover pan, and let stand 5 minutes until cheese partially melts. Sprinkle lightly with mace, if you wish.

Portuguese Sausage Soup

⏱ *Preparation time: 10 minutes. Cooking time: 30 minutes*

Potatoes, spinach, and sausage make this a sturdy soup, worthy of top billing for a cold-weather supper. Hot cornbread would go well with it; so would a salad of shredded carrots.

    2 medium-size potatoes, peeled and thinly sliced
       (about 1 lb.)
    1 medium-size onion, thinly sliced
    1 can (about 14 oz.) regular-strength chicken
       broth
    ½ cup water
    ⅛ teaspoon pepper
    ¾ pound spinach
    ½ pound linguisa or chorizo sausage
       Boiling water
    1 tablespoon butter or margarine

In a 3-quart pan, combine potatoes, onion, broth, the ½ cup water, and pepper; bring to a boil, reduce heat, cover, and simmer until vegetables are fork tender (about 25 minutes).

Meanwhile, remove and discard spinach stems; rinse leaves well, drain, and cut into very fine, short shreds. Set aside. Place sausage in a frying pan with about ½ inch boiling water; simmer, covered, for 15 minutes. Drain, remove casing, and cut into thin slanting slices or crumble; set aside.

Whirl potato mixture in a blender or food processor until smooth; return puréed mixture to pan. Add butter and spinach and cook over low heat, uncovered, for about 3 minutes or until greens are wilted but still bright green. Stir in reserved sausage and heat through.

Eggplant Supper Soup

⏱ *Preparation time: 10 minutes. Cooking time: 40 minutes*

Another full-meal soup, starring ground beef, can be made in less than an hour and you can ignore it for about half of that time.

    1 tablespoon olive oil or salad oil
    1 tablespoon butter or margarine
    1 small onion, chopped
    ½ pound lean ground beef
    1 small eggplant (about 1 lb.), diced
    1 small clove garlic, minced or pressed
    1 small carrot, shredded
    1 can (14 oz.) pear-shaped tomatoes
    1 can (about 14 oz.) regular-strength beef broth
    ½ teaspoon *each* salt and sugar
    ¼ teaspoon *each* pepper and ground nutmeg
    2 tablespoons *each* salad macaroni and minced
       parsley
       Grated Parmesan cheese

Heat oil and butter in a 3-quart pan over medium heat; add onion and cook, stirring, until limp. Crumble meat into pan and stir over medium-high heat until it loses its pinkness. Skim off and discard fat. Add eggplant, garlic, carrot, tomatoes (breaking them up with a spoon) and their liquid, beef broth, salt, sugar, pepper, and nutmeg. Cover and simmer for about 30 minutes.

Add macaroni and parsley and simmer for 10 to 15 minutes more or until macaroni is tender to bite. Pass cheese to sprinkle over servings.

Spinach Meatball Minestrone

⏱ *Preparation time: 20 minutes. Cooking time: 25 minutes*

A good choice for a busy day, spinach meatball minestrone tastes as if it takes hours to make.

       Spinach meatballs (recipe follows)
       Butter or margarine
    1 can (14 oz.) regular-strength beef broth
    1 can (8 oz.) stewed tomatoes
    1 can (8 oz.) kidney beans
    ¼ teaspoon *each* oregano leaves and dry basil
    ¼ cup *each* sliced carrot and celery
    ¼ cup elbow or bow-shaped macaroni
       Parmesan cheese

(Continued on next page)

In a wide frying pan, brown meatballs in butter, if needed, over medium heat; remove from pan as browned.

In a 3-quart pan, pour beef broth, tomatoes (breaking up with a spoon) and their liquid, beans and their liquid, oregano, basil, carrot, celery, and meatballs. Cover and bring to a boil. Reduce heat and cook over medium heat for 15 minutes or until vegetables are tender and meatballs cooked through; skim off any accumulated fat.

Stir in macaroni, cover, and cook until tender to bite (about 10 minutes). Sprinkle servings with Parmesan cheese.

Spinach meatballs. Squeeze liquid from 1 package (10 oz.) **frozen chopped spinach,** thawed; mix with ½ pound **lean ground beef,** 2 tablespoons **fine dry bread crumbs,** 1 **egg,** ¼ teaspoon **salt,** dash **pepper,** and 1 small **onion,** finely chopped. Shape into 1-inch balls.

Greek Meatball Soup

🕐 *Preparation time: 15 minutes. Cooking time: 30 minutes*

Tiny meatballs simmer in the stock of this hearty supper soup, which cooks in less than 45 minutes. With it, nibble crisp Armenian cracker bread or bread sticks.

- 1 **tablespoon butter or margarine**
- 1 **medium-size onion, finely chopped**
- 2 **cans (14 oz. each) regular-strength beef broth**
- ½ **pound lean ground beef**
- 1 **tablespoon rice**
- 1 **small clove garlic, minced or pressed**
- ¼ **teaspoon salt**
- ⅛ **teaspoon oregano leaves, crumbled**
- ⅓ **cup finely chopped parsley**
- 1 **tablespoon cornstarch blended with 2 tablespoons cold water**
- ⅓ **cup each whipping cream and shredded Parmesan cheese**
  Chopped green onions
  Shredded Parmesan cheese

Melt butter in a 3-quart pan. Add onion and cook, stirring, over medium heat until limp. Remove ⅓ of the onion from pan and set aside. Add beef broth to pan; cover and simmer while shaping meatballs.

Mix together ground beef, reserved sautéed onion, rice, garlic, salt, and oregano; shape into marble-size balls. Roll in parsley and drop into bubbling broth. Cover and simmer for 25 minutes.

Stir cornstarch mixture into simmering soup. Mix together cream and the ⅓ cup Parmesan; ladle about ½ cup hot broth into cheese mixture, stirring constantly; then return to pan, stirring. Cook and stir a few minutes longer until soup boils and thickens slightly. Pass small bowls of green onion and Parmesan cheese to spoon over.

Maritata Soup

🕐 *Preparation time (cooking included): 15 minutes*

Use either canned broth or your own homemade broth to make this Italian soup. When you serve it as a light main dish, add crusty bread, a salad such as Belgian endive with a tart dressing, and a fruit dessert.

- 4 **cups regular-strength beef or chicken broth**
- 1 **to 2 ounces vermicelli**
- ¼ **cup unsalted butter, at room temperature**
- ⅓ **cup freshly grated Parmesan cheese**
- 2 **egg yolks**
- ½ **cup whipping cream**

Bring broth to a boil in a 2 to 3-quart pan. Add vermicelli (broken into shorter lengths, if you wish) and boil, uncovered, for 7 to 9 minutes or until tender to bite. Meanwhile, in a bowl blend butter with cheese and egg yolks, then gradually beat in cream. Spoon a little hot broth into cream mixture, stirring constantly; then return to pan and cook, stirring constantly, until heated through.

Chopstick Soups

Some very satisfying whole-meal soups can start with an easy-to-fix Oriental noodle soup mix. The package contains precooked noodles that take only 2 or 3 minutes to prepare, a packet of soup base for the broth, and sometimes other seasonings. Look for packages among the Oriental foods in your market.

You can also buy Oriental-style noodles alone—combine them with canned broth and some interesting ingredients of your own (several suggestions follow), and you'll probably find that your creations are the best of all.

Understanding the labels

Before you shop, make at least a mental note of these four definitions; they'll help you understand the often confusing package labels.

The word *mein* (pronounced *meen*, incidentally) is a general Chinese name for noodles. The Japanese word *somem* means thin, round noodles, and *udon* is the word for wide, flat ones. *Saimin* is Hawaii's version of noodle soup.

Because most Oriental noodles contain no egg—and U. S. Government regulations require that egg be an ingredient in a product labeled noodles—the Oriental products are often called alimentary paste or imitation noodles.

Most soup mixes have cooking directions in English; on those that don't, you'll often find guidance in the form of little drawings. Each package makes at least one generous serving, but it will serve two people if you add bits of cooked meats, eggs, fish, or vegetables.

It's fun to serve the soup with chopsticks (for eating the noodles, meat, and vegetables) and an Oriental or regular soup spoon for the broth.

Making the noodle part...

With or without a mix, it's only a matter of minutes from empty pan to fragrant, noodle-filled, bubbling broth.

To make noodle soup from a mix, follow directions on the package. If the directions aren't readable, do this: Bring 2 to 3 cups salted water to a boil, add noodles, and boil until tender (usually 2 or 3 minutes). Add soup base and about 1 cup of any cooked meats and vegetables you choose; stir and heat through. Remove from heat and serve in large soup bowls, arranging some of the colorful added ingredients attractively on top. Sprinkle with sliced green onion, minced parsley, or chopped fresh coriander (cilantro), if you wish.

To make noodle soup from scratch, cook 2 to 3 ounces Oriental noodles, regular noodles, or vermicelli in 2 to 3 cups boiling salted water until just tender to bite (start testing in about 2 minutes, as some cook quickly); drain. Heat 1 can (about 14 oz.) regular-strength chicken broth or beef broth to boiling, add drained noodles, 1 teaspoon soy sauce, and about 1 cup meat or vegetables of your choice (suggestions follow). Heat through and serve as directed above.

...and adding the zest

Think in terms of combinations of the following ingredients (all cut into bite-size pieces), and the possibilities for adding flavor and texture become almost infinite.

Cooked meats, such as beef, pork, ham, or lamb; Chinese barbecued pork (called *chahr siu*, available in Oriental stores); chicken, turkey, or duck.

Fish and shellfish, such as cooked or canned fish, shrimp, crab, clams, or abalone; Japanese steamed fish cake (called *kamaboko*), sliced.

Eggs, hard-cooked, sliced, and arranged on top of soup just before serving. Or drop a raw egg (or just the yolk) into center of bowl of hot soup and swirl through for flavor.

Vegetables, such as cooked carrots, green beans, celery, mushrooms, soaked dried mushrooms. Or add raw spinach leaves, Chinese cabbage, Chinese edible pod peas, or bean sprouts to the boiling water and cook briefly along with the noodles.

SALADS

"Let's just have a salad to-night." This is a frequent rallying cry among people accustomed to business lunches, concerned about diet, living with irregular dinner hours, too busy to stop and "cook" dinner.

It's a boon to be able to grab ingredients from the cupboard or refrigerator and combine them with fresh lettuce or other salad greens or fresh fruit for a quick and wonderful meal. One trick is to keep cans of tuna, salmon, crab, ham, and shrimp on hand. Another is to have sliced meats from the deli in your freezer to pull out for last-minute use. An assortment of cheeses will also be useful, along with citrus fruits and raisins—these foods take to relatively long storage and do great things for salads.

The recipes in this chapter offer a taste of Mexico, the Orient, and Vietnam, as well as more typically American pairing of such ingredients as ham and turkey, chicken and fruit.

Few foods have more visual appeal or more variations than salads. They can be the focal point of any meal, hearty enough to stand on their own; they can share the spotlight with soup and crusty French bread; or they can be simply the crisp, fresh prelude, postlude, or accompaniment to a meal that features a more elaborate entrée.

Ham and Turkey Salad

Preparation time (cooking included): 20 minutes.
Chilling time: 15 minutes

A curry-flavored dressing distinguishes this attractive salad. Complement it with hot corn muffins.

- ½ cup slivered almonds
- 1½ cups diced cooked turkey
- ½ cup diced cooked ham (or cut in matchstick-size pieces)
- 1 small red-skinned apple
- 2 teaspoons lemon juice
- ½ cup *each* seedless grapes and mayonnaise
- ¾ teaspoon soy sauce
- ½ teaspoon curry powder
  Crisp salad greens
  Small grape clusters (optional)

Spread almonds in a shallow pan and toast in a 350° oven for 8 to 10 minutes or until golden; set aside.

Combine turkey, ham, and ⅓ cup of the toasted almonds. Core and thinly slice apple and coat with lemon juice; add to meat. Stir in the ½ cup grapes. Blend mayonnaise with soy and curry; pour over salad. Press into a 4 to 5-cup bowl, cover, and chill at least 15 minutes. Turn out on a bed of greens. Garnish with remaining toasted almonds and surround with grape clusters, if you wish.

Mexican Mixed Salad

Preparation time: 15 minutes

Chef's salad, Mexican-style, combines julienne strips of meat or chicken with typical flavors from south of the border—chili, coriander, lime. You serve it with avocado and orange slices on a bed of shredded lettuce.

- 1 large orange
  About 3 cups shredded iceberg lettuce
- 4 green onions, finely chopped
- 6 ounces sliced cooked ham, chicken or turkey breast, tongue, or rare roast beef
- 3 tablespoons olive oil or salad oil
- 1½ teaspoons white wine vinegar
- 2 teaspoons lime or lemon juice
- 1 clove garlic, minced or pressed
- ¼ teaspoon *each* sugar, chili powder, and ground coriander
- 1 small avocado, peeled, pitted, and sliced
  Pitted ripe olives

Cut peel and white membrane from orange and cut orange into thin slices; set aside. Mix lettuce with onions. Cut meat into julienne strips and mix half into greens. Stir together oil, vinegar, lime juice, garlic, sugar, chili powder, and coriander; pour dressing over greens and toss lightly. Mound in center of a rimmed platter (about 9 inches in diameter). Arrange remaining meat strips on top of greens. Arrange avocado and orange slices around base. Garnish with olives.

Tostada

🕐 *Preparation time (cooking included): 15 minutes*

Pile high this meaty Mexican salad and surround it with crisp tortilla chips.

½ **pound lean ground beef**
1 **small onion, chopped**
1 **can (8 oz.) red kidney beans, drained**
¾ **teaspoon chili powder**
¼ **teaspoon ground cumin**
3 **tablespoons catsup**
  About 3 cups shredded iceberg lettuce
½ **cup shredded jack cheese**
1 **medium-size tomato, cut in wedges**
  Tortilla chips

Crumble meat into an 8 or 9-inch frying pan, add onion, and cook, stirring, over medium heat until meat has lost its pink color and onion is limp; drain and discard excess fat. Add kidney beans, chili powder, cumin, and catsup; simmer gently, covered, for about 5 minutes to blend flavors.

Meanwhile, arrange lettuce on 2 dinner plates. Top lettuce with hot beef mixture, sprinkle with cheese, and garnish with tomato wedges and tortilla chips. Pass additional chips at table.

Roast Beef and Crab Salad

🕐 *Preparation time: 10 minutes. Chilling time: 15 minutes*

Rare roast beef and crab may seem like an odd couple, but they team up deliciously with creamy tarragon dressing, and the result is an unusual and filling salad.

For each serving, arrange outer leaves of **butter lettuce** on a plate; tear several additional leaves and mound in center of plate. Arrange 3 or 4 thin slices rare **roast beef** (about ¼ lb.) folded in half, several chunks of **crab meat** (about 2 oz.), 3 sliced **mushrooms,** 6 **cherry tomatoes,** ¼ cup canned **garbanzos,** ½-ounce chunk **blue cheese** or Roquefort (crumbled), and 3 **marinated artichoke hearts.** Cover and chill at least 15 minutes. Spoon over **tarragon dressing** (recipe follows). Makes 1 serving.

Tarragon dressing. Blend together ¼ cup *each* **sour cream** and **mayonnaise.** Stir in 1 tablespoon **lemon juice,** ¼ teaspoon crumbled **tarragon leaves,** and ⅛ teaspoon *each* **dry mustard** and **garlic salt.** Makes ½ cup.

Salmon Salad with Oranges

🕐 *Preparation time: 10 minutes*

Canned salmon goes together quickly with fresh orange sections and tangy sour cream dressing.

1 **can (about 8 oz.) salmon, drained**
1½ **cups thinly sliced celery**
⅓ **cup thinly sliced green onion**
2 **tablespoons finely chopped parsley**
¼ **cup thinly sliced pimento-stuffed green olives**
2 **large oranges**
  Tangy dressing (recipe follows)
  Lettuce leaves
  Sliced pimento-stuffed green olives

Turn salmon into a bowl, discard skin and bones, and break salmon into bite-size pieces. Add celery, onion, parsley, and the ¼ cup olives. Mix together lightly; chill for at least 15 minutes.

Just before serving, peel oranges and remove all white membrane. Separate orange sections and set a few aside for garnish; cut remaining sections in half and add to salmon.

Lightly toss salad with tangy dressing and serve on lettuce-lined plates. Garnish with reserved orange sections and sliced green olives.

(Continued on next page)

SALADS **11**

Tangy dressing. Mix together 3 tablespoons *each* **sour cream** and **mayonnaise**, 1 teaspoon *each* **Dijon mustard** and **prepared horseradish**, ½ teaspoon **garlic salt**, ⅛ teaspoon **pepper**, and 1 teaspoon grated **orange peel.**

Hot Chicken Salad

⏱ *Preparation time (cooking included): 10 minutes*

For a light and low-calorie meal, serve this hot chicken salad adapted from a classic Chinese recipe. Add the warm and well-seasoned chicken at the very end to keep the lettuce crisp.

> 2 teaspoons *each* sesame seeds, prepared
>   mustard, and lemon juice
> 2 tablespoons regular-strength chicken broth or
>   water
> ¼ teaspoon *each* salt, sugar, and ground coriander
> ¼ cup chopped green onion
> 1½ cups diced or shredded cooked chicken or
>   turkey
>   About 2 cups shredded iceberg lettuce

Toast sesame seed in a frying pan over medium heat until golden, stirring frequently. Stir in mustard, lemon juice, chicken broth, salt, sugar, coriander, and onion. Add chicken and heat through. Arrange shredded lettuce on a warm platter and spoon hot chicken mixture over.

Tuna and Fruit Salad

⏱ *Preparation time (cooking included): 15 minutes.*
Chilling time: 30 minutes

A combination of shell macaroni, fruit, tuna, and toasted almonds tossed with a curry dressing makes a very special seafood salad.

> ½ cup small shell macaroni
>   Boiling salted water
> 1 large apple, cored and diced
> 2½ tablespoons lemon juice
> 1 cup sliced celery
> ½ cup raisins or halved seeded grapes
> ¼ cup thinly sliced green onion
> 1 can (6½ oz.) tuna, drained
> ½ cup mayonnaise
> 1½ teaspoons curry powder
> 1 teaspoon Dijon mustard
>   Salt
> ⅓ cup sliced almonds
>   Lettuce leaves

Cook macaroni in boiling salted water as directed on package; drain and chill. Meanwhile, mix together apple, lemon juice, celery, raisins, onion, and tuna (breaking it apart with a fork).

Combine mayonnaise, curry powder, and mustard. Mix into salad gently; salt to taste. Cover and chill for at least 30 minutes.

Spread almonds in a shallow pan and toast in a 350° oven for 8 to 10 minutes or until golden; set aside.

Mix macaroni and half the almonds into salad. Serve salad on lettuce-lined plates with remaining almonds sprinkled on top.

Dilled Shrimp Salad

⏱ *Preparation time: 10 minutes. Marinating time: 1 hour*

Tiny pink shrimp marinate in a dill dressing. At the last minute you toss greens and cheese cubes with the shrimp and dressing—and there's dinner.

> 3 tablespoons olive oil or salad oil
> 2 teaspoons white wine vinegar
> 1 teaspoon lemon juice
> ¼ teaspoon *each* dill weed and Dijon mustard
> ⅛ teaspoon salt
>   Dash *each* garlic powder and pepper
> ½ pound small cooked shrimp
> 1½ cups *each* torn romaine and butter lettuce
>   leaves
> ¼ cup cubed Tilsit or jack cheese

In a small jar, combine oil, vinegar, lemon juice, dill weed, mustard, salt, garlic powder, and pepper; shake well to blend. Pour over shrimp; cover and refrigerate for about 1 hour, or until serving time.

Mix shrimp mixture lightly with greens and cheese.

Creamy Chicken with Oranges

⏱ *Preparation time (cooking included): 30 minutes.*
Chilling time: 2 hours

A mound of orange-flavored chicken chunks on a lettuce leaf are topped with thin slices of orange and toasted almonds. Accompany with crisp bread sticks.

  1 **large whole chicken breast (about 1½ lb.), split**
      Boiling salted water
  ¼ **cup slivered almonds, toasted (directions follow)**
  ⅓ **cup sliced celery**
  2 **tablespoons** *each* **chopped green onion and green pepper**
  1 **large orange**
  ¼ **cup** *each* **sour cream and mayonnaise**
1½ **teaspoons** *each* **sugar and lemon juice**
      Salt and pepper
      Crisp salad greens

In a wide frying pan, place chicken breast in about 1 inch boiling salted water; cover, reduce heat, and simmer for about 15 minutes or until meat is no longer

pink inside. Let cool to touch. Discard skin and bones and cut meat into chunks—you should have about 2 cups.

Spread almonds in a shallow pan and toast in a 350° oven for 8 to 10 minutes or until golden; set aside.

Combine chicken, celery, onion, and green pepper. Grate ½ teaspoon orange peel; set aside. Remove remaining peel and white membrane, then thinly slice orange; cover and refrigerate. Blend sour cream, mayonnaise, sugar, lemon juice, reserved orange peel, and salt and pepper to taste. Stir into chicken mixture, cover, and chill for 2 to 3 hours.

To serve, place salad greens on individual serving plates; top with chicken mixture and garnish with reserved orange slices and almonds.

Vegetable Antipasto Salad

⏱ *Preparation time (cooking included): 30 minutes.*
Chilling time: 2 hours

Traditionally served as appetizers, colorful antipasto vegetables can also become a tempting, chilled, whole-meal salad—appropriate for lunch or a light supper. Cooked just long enough to absorb an herb-flavored tomato sauce, the crisp vegetables are accompanied by sardines and hard-cooked egg wedges.

  1 **cup tomato-based chili sauce**
  ¼ **cup** *each* **olive oil and lemon juice**
  1 **teaspoon** *each* **oregano leaves and prepared horseradish**
  1 **clove garlic, minced or pressed**
  2 **stalks celery, cut in ¾-inch-wide chunks**
  1 **large green pepper, seeded and cut in ½-inch-wide strips**
  2 **medium-size zucchini, cut in ¼-inch-thick slices**
  1 **jar (8 oz.) peperoncini**
      Lettuce leaves
      Sliced pimento-stuffed green olives
  2 **hard-cooked eggs, cut in wedges**
  1 **can (3¾ oz.) sardines, packed in oil (drained)**

In a wide frying pan, combine chili sauce, olive oil, lemon juice, oregano, horseradish, and garlic; cook for several minutes over medium heat.

Add celery, green pepper, zucchini, and peperoncini; simmer, uncovered, until vegetables are fork tender (about 12 minutes), stirring often. Cover and chill 2 to 4 hours—vegetables should be cold.

Lift vegetables from sauce with slotted spoon and mound on 2 lettuce-lined plates. Top each with 2 tablespoons sauce and garnish with sliced olives. Arrange hard-cooked egg wedges and sardines along one side of each plate.

Marinated Mushroom Salad

⏱ *Preparation time: 10 minutes. Marinating time: 1 hour*

By itself, this marinated fresh mushroom salad is filling enough to make a light meal. But when combined with a cup of soup, it's a dinner delight. Chunks of zesty blue cheese and crunchy walnuts sprinkled over make an attractive serving. (See photograph on page 34.)

¼ cup olive oil or salad oil
2 teaspoons dry basil
½ teaspoon salt
⅛ teaspoon *each* pepper and paprika
2 teaspoons Dijon mustard
4 teaspoons white wine vinegar
1 teaspoon lemon juice
½ pound mushrooms, sliced
½ cup thinly sliced green onion, including some green tops
¾ cup broken walnut pieces (optional)
About 4 ounces blue cheese, coarsely crumbled
3 cups torn chicory (curly endive), romaine, or butter lettuce leaves
About 6 cherry tomatoes, whole or halved

In a salad bowl, combine oil, basil, salt, pepper, paprika, mustard, vinegar, and lemon juice. Beat with a fork until blended. Mix in mushrooms and green onion; marinate at room temperature for about 1 hour or until serving time.

Mix in walnut pieces, blue cheese, chicory, and cherry tomatoes. Or serve mushrooms on a lettuce-lined plate and garnish with walnut pieces, blue cheese, and cherry tomatoes.

Swiss Cheese Vegetable Salad

⏱ *Preparation time: 10 minutes. Chilling time: 1 to 3 hours*

Let vegetables marinate an hour in the piquant Italian herb dressing before combining with matchstick-size Swiss cheese pieces. Serve for a summer brunch or light supper.

1 small can (8 oz.) garbanzo beans, drained
1 small can (8 oz.) red kidney beans, drained
About ½ head cauliflower, sliced ½ inch thick (about 1¼ cups)
1 zucchini (about 6 oz.) sliced ⅛ inch thick
1 small mild red onion, thinly sliced
Italian herb dressing (recipe follows)
4 to 6 ounces Jarlsberg, jack, or Swiss cheese

In a bowl, mix garbanzo beans, kidney beans, cauliflower, zucchini, and onion. Add Italian herb dressing and mix lightly. Cover and refrigerate for 1 to 3 hours.

Cut cheese in matchstick-size pieces and mix into salad before serving.

Italian herb dressing. In a jar, mix together well 6 tablespoons **olive oil** or salad oil, ¼ cup **red wine vinegar**, 1 small clove **garlic** (minced or pressed), ¾ teaspoon **salt** (or to taste), ½ teaspoon **sugar**, ½ teaspoon **Italian herb seasoning** (or ¼ teaspoon *each* oregano leaves and dry basil), and ¼ teaspoon **pepper.**

Peanut and Tofu-filled Pineapple Boats

⏱ *Preparation time: 20 minutes*

Tofu puffs and peanuts supply the protein in this salad. A pineapple shell holds the salad, all dressed up in a spicy peanut butter sauce. Look for deep-fried tofu puffs in Oriental markets.

1 large pineapple (4 to 5 lb.)
1 small cucumber, thinly sliced
¼ pound bean sprouts
2 tablespoons thinly sliced green onion
½ cup sliced canned water chestnuts
About 1½ ounces Japanese-style deep-fried tofu puffs, cut in ¾-inch cubes, or 5 ounces Chinese-style tofu puffs
Peanut sauce (recipe follows)
¼ cup coarsely chopped salted peanuts

Cut pineapple lengthwise through stem. With a grapefruit knife, cut around edge of each half, leaving sides about ½ inch thick. Lift out fruit, cut away core, and cut fruit in ¾-inch cubes to make about 2 cups. Drain shells.

Just before serving, drain pineapple cubes; mix together with cucumber, bean sprouts, onion, water chestnuts, tofu, and peanut sauce. Spoon into pineapple shells and sprinkle with peanuts.

Peanut sauce. Stir together ⅓ cup **chunk-style peanut butter,** 3 tablespoons firmly-packed **brown sugar,** ¼ to ½ teaspoon crushed **red pepper,** and ¼ cup **lemon juice.**

Nicoise Supper Salad

⏱ *Preparation time: 10 minutes*

This classic salad can be made in many ways. Tuna is skirted by tomato, olives, hard-cooked egg, and crisp vegetables. Then everything is dressed with anchovy. For variation, try stuffing Arab pocket (peda) bread with the salad makings for hearty sandwiches. (See photograph on page 26.)

> **Butter lettuce**
> 1 **small can (6½ oz.) chunk-style tuna, drained**
> 2 **hard-cooked eggs, halved or quartered**
> 1 **large tomato, cut in wedges**
> 1 **small green pepper, seeded and slivered**
> ½ **medium-size mild red onion, cut in rounds**
> 1 **stalk celery, thinly sliced**
> ½ **cup pitted black or green olives, drained**
> 4 **large mushrooms, thinly sliced (optional)**
> 1 **jar (6 oz.) marinated artichoke hearts, drained**
> **Alfalfa sprouts (optional)**
> **Canned miniature corn on the cob, drained**
> **Anchovies, drained**
> **Niçoise dressing (recipe follows)**
> **Arab pocket bread (optional)**

Line a rimmed platter with butter lettuce. Place tuna in center. Around it group eggs, tomato, green pepper, onion, celery, and olives. If you like, also add mushrooms, artichoke hearts, alfalfa sprouts, miniature corn on the cob, and anchovies. Just before serving, moisten evenly with about half the dressing, then pass remaining dressing to serve over. Or stuff Arab pocket bread halves with any ingredients above.

Niçoise dressing. Blend 2 teaspoons *each* minced canned **anchovies** and **Dijon mustard** with 3 tablespoons **wine vinegar** and 5 tablespoons **olive oil.**

Curried Egg and Shrimp-stuffed Tomatoes

⏱ *Preparation time: 10 minutes. Chilling time: 20 minutes*

Partially sliced tomatoes have nifty pockets for a stuffing of egg and shrimp. Decorate with toasted almonds. (See cover photograph.)

> 1½ **tablespoons mayonnaise**
> ¼ **teaspoon curry powder**
> ⅛ **teaspoon garlic salt**
> **Dash cayenne**
> 2 **hard-cooked eggs, chopped**
> 1 **tablespoon chopped green onion**
> 2 **tablespoons chopped celery**
> ⅛ **pound small cooked shrimp, coarsely chopped**
> 1 **tablespoon sliced or slivered almonds**
> 2 **medium-size firm, ripe tomatoes**
> **Lettuce leaves**

Mix together mayonnaise, curry powder, garlic salt, cayenne, chopped eggs, green onion, and celery. Cover and chill up to 24 hours. Add shrimp just before ready to serve.

Spread almonds in a shallow pan and toast in a 350° oven for 8 minutes or until golden; set aside.

To peel tomatoes, dip in boiling water 45 seconds, rinse in cold water, and slip off skins. Cut out stems.

Cut each tomato into 4 or 5 slices without cutting all the way through to stem.

Place tomatoes on lettuce-lined salad plates. Gently open slices and fill with several spoonfuls egg-shrimp mixture. Cover and chill for at least 20 minutes. Sprinkle with toasted almonds.

Basic Salad Dressings

These two old favorite dressings will stay fresh in the refrigerator 2 to 3 weeks. Toss with your favorite salad greens.

Vinaigrette Dressing

Mash 2 hard-cooked **egg yolks** to a paste with ¼ cup **malt vinegar** or cider vinegar. Gradually blend in 6 tablespoons **salad oil.** Stir in 2 finely chopped **green onions** and add **salt** and **coarsely ground pepper** to taste; mix well. Makes about ¾ cup.

Creamy Louis Dressing

Stir together 1 cup **mayonnaise,** ⅓ cup **sweet pickle relish,** 3 tablespoons finely chopped **green pepper,** and ⅛ teaspoon **liquid hot pepper seasoning.** Whip ½ cup **whipping cream** until stiff; gently fold into mayonnaise mixture until thoroughly blended. Cover and chill. Makes about 2 cups dressing.

SANDWICHES

A sandwich can be anything tucked between, placed atop, or rolled inside bread slices, buns, tortillas, crisp rye crackers, Arab pocket bread, or even a paper-thin omelet. Being innovative is half the fun.

Lots of hearty open-faced and closed sandwiches, filling enough for any meal, are here to enjoy. Making them doesn't require lots of forethought, and you get all the credit for the imagination. Serve them alone or with soup or salad.

Tuna Sandwiches with Bean Sprouts

⏱ *Preparation time: 10 minutes*

Fresh bean sprouts add crunch to a tuna spread that's great on toasted English muffins. With a pair of these and some raw vegetables, you're all set for Saturday lunch.

2 English muffins
   Butter or margarine
1 cup bean sprouts
1 can (6½ oz.) tuna, drained
¼ cup mayonnaise
2 tablespoons minced parsley
⅓ cup chopped dill pickle
¼ cup *each* chopped green pepper and sliced green onion (including some tops)
1 hard-cooked egg, cut in slices
   Dill pickle slices
   Radishes

Split and toast English muffins and spread with butter. Scatter bean sprouts over muffins.

Mix together tuna, mayonnaise, parsley, pickle, green pepper, and onion. Heap on top of bean sprouts. Top each sandwich with slices of hard-cooked egg. Garnish each plate with a dill pickle slice and some radishes. Makes 2 sandwiches.

Zucchini and Egg Sandwiches

⏱ *Preparation time: 10 minutes*

You can eat this as a closed sandwich or open-faced. Crisp zucchini and egg slices make it a satisfying, wholesome meal.

3 tablespoons mayonnaise
1 clove garlic, minced or pressed
¼ teaspoon *each* salt, pepper, and prepared horseradish
2 small zucchini, thinly sliced
   Butter or margarine
2 to 4 slices pumpernickel, rye, or whole wheat bread
   Butter lettuce leaves
2 tablespoons thinly sliced green onion
1 hard-cooked egg, sliced

Mix together mayonnaise, garlic, salt, pepper, and prepared horseradish until blended. Stir in zucchini.

If you'd like open-faced sandwiches, just butter one side of 2 slices of bread. On each buttered slice, lay lettuce leaf . Then spoon half the zucchini mixture over each sandwich and sprinkle each with half the green onion. Arrange half the hard-cooked egg slices on each. Serve open-faced or top with an additional slice of buttered bread for a closed sandwich. Makes 2 sandwiches.

Curried Tuna-Apple Sandwiches

🕐 *Preparation time: 10 minutes*

Curry lifts "good old tuna" above the ordinary, especially with bits of crisp apple and raisins contributing sweetness. Toasted raisin bread is the ideal base for these open-faced sandwiches.

- ¼ **cup mayonnaise**
- ½ **teaspoon curry powder**
- ¼ **teaspoon garlic salt**
- **Dash cayenne**
- 1 **tablespoon lemon juice**
- 1 **can (6½ oz.) chunk-style tuna, drained**
- ¾ **cup chopped apple**
- ½ **cup finely chopped celery**
- ¼ **cup raisins**
- 2 **tablespoons thinly sliced green onion (including some tops)**
- **Butter or margarine**
- 4 **slices raisin bread or whole wheat bread**
- **Alfalfa sprouts (optional)**

Mix together mayonnaise, curry powder, garlic salt, cayenne, and lemon juice. Stir in tuna, apple, celery, raisins, and onion until blended.

Toast and butter bread; spread equal portions of tuna mixture over each sandwich, then sprinkle with alfalfa sprouts, if you wish. Makes 4 sandwiches or 2 servings.

Salmon Sandwiches with Egg

🕐 *Preparation time: 10 minutes*

A knife-and-fork sandwich that's ready in minutes is this nourishing one made from canned salmon.

Cut 4 thin center slices from 2 **hard-cooked eggs** and reserve for garnish. In a bowl, chop remaining egg and combine with 2 tablespoons **mayonnaise.** Spread egg mixture on 2 slices **whole wheat bread.** Top egg with sprigs of **watercress.** Drain 1 can (about 7 oz.) **salmon;** discard skin and bones, break salmon into chunks, and arrange evenly over cress. Garnish with egg slices. Makes 2 sandwiches.

Smoked Salmon Sandwiches

🕐 *Preparation time: 10 minutes*

Arrange slices of smoked salmon over crisp cucumber slices and cream cheese for a pumpernickel special.

- 1 **small package (3 oz.) cream cheese, softened**
- 1 **teaspoon lemon juice**
- 2 **slices pumpernickel bread**
- 12 **cucumber slices**
- 1 **package (3½ oz.) sliced smoked salmon**
- **Chopped green onion**

Mix together until blended the cream cheese and lemon juice. Spread cream cheese over pumpernickel bread. Arrange half the cucumber slices on each sandwich and top with equal amounts of the smoked salmon. Garnish salmon with chopped green onion. Makes 2 sandwiches.

Ham and Cheese with Coleslaw

🕐 *Preparation time (cooking included): 10 minutes*

Sandwich and salad are all one when you top ham and melted cheese with a generous serving of coleslaw. Carrot curls and tomato wedges are the final touch.

For each sandwich, toast 2 slices **rye bread** or split and toast an English muffin; spread with **butter** or margarine and **prepared mustard** to taste. Top each

with a slice of cooked **ham** and a slice of **Cheddar cheese** (about 2 oz. of *each*) and place under broiler until cheese melts. Top generously with **coleslaw** (homemade or purchased) and garnish with **tomato wedges** and **carrot** curls. Makes 1 sandwich.

Egg Crêpe Sandwiches

⏱ *Preparation time (cooking included): 10 minutes*

Eggs cook in a thin layer to form a crêpe, which you top with cheese and chili powder, then roll up and tuck inside a toasted bun.

Split 2 sandwich-size **French rolls** or hot dog buns, spread lightly with **butter** or margarine, and toast cut surfaces in a wide frying pan over medium heat. Remove from pan and keep warm.

Lightly beat together 3 **eggs.** Melt 1 teaspoon **butter** or margarine in pan over medium heat; tilt pan to coat bottom. Add half the beaten egg; quickly tilt pan to form a thin, even layer over bottom. Sprinkle ¾ cup shredded **Cheddar cheese** and 1 teaspoon **Mexican seasoning** or chili powder over egg. When egg is lightly browned on bottom, remove from heat. With a wide spatula, roll egg up, fold in half, and place in **French roll** (leave unfolded for hot dog bun). Repeat with remaining egg. Makes 2 sandwiches.

Roast Beef Mushroom Sandwich

⏱ *Preparation time: 10 minutes*

A mushroom-laden sandwich of rare roast beef can be topped with tomato wedges and a spoonful of creamy blue cheese dressing, if you like. (See photograph on facing page.)

For each sandwich, lightly toast 2 slices **corn rye bread** or split French rolls and spread with **mayonnaise** and **Dijon mustard** to taste. Place toast slices side by side on plate and cover each with several **lettuce** leaves. Top evenly with about 3 ounces thinly sliced rare **roast beef.** Sprinkle over meat 2 or 3 thinly sliced raw **mushrooms** and 2 to 3 thin slices of

A PORTABLE SOUP AND SANDWICH supper: quick gazpacho served in chilled mugs (page 5) and a roast beef sandwich stacked high with meat, sliced mushrooms, onion rings, and tomato wedges (recipe above). Finish meal with individual raspberry tarts (page 77).

mild onion, separated into rings. Season with **salt** and **pepper,** and garnish with **tomato wedges** and **ripe olives.** Spoon over **blue cheese dressing** or Italian-style dressing, if you wish. Makes 1 sandwich.

Toasted Jack Cheese and Mushroom Sandwiches

⏱ *Preparation time (cooking included): 10 minutes*

Sautéed mushrooms, tomatoes, and cheese top this open-faced sandwich. Serve it hot from the broiler with a cup of onion soup for a quick lunch or supper.

    About 3 tablespoons butter or margarine
½ **pound mushrooms, sliced**
4 **slices light rye bread**
2 **medium-size tomatoes, peeled and sliced**
6 **ounces jack cheese, sliced**
    Parsley sprigs

In a wide frying pan over medium heat, melt 2 tablespoons of the butter; add mushrooms and cook until liquid evaporates. Toast bread, butter lightly, place on a baking sheet, and cover each slice with a layer of mushrooms, reserving ⅓ of them for garnish. Evenly arrange a layer of tomatoes atop mushrooms; cover evenly with cheese. Broil about 4 inches from heat until cheese melts. Spoon over reserved mushrooms and garnish with parsley sprigs. Makes 4 sandwiches or 2 servings.

Chicken Supper Sandwiches

⏱ *Preparation time (cooking included): 30 minutes*

You'll need a knife and fork to eat these towering open-faced chicken sandwiches. Accompany them with an assortment of crisp raw vegetables.

1 **whole chicken breast (about 1 lb.)**
    Salted water
4 **slices bacon**
2 **English muffins, split, toasted, and buttered**
4 **slices mild red onion**
1 **large tomato, peeled and cut into 4 thick slices**
½ **cup shredded Longhorn Cheddar cheese**

Simmer chicken in a small amount of salted water until meat is no longer pink throughout (about 15 minutes); drain, discard skin and bones, and slice meat.

(Continued on next page)

Meanwhile cut bacon slices in half crosswise and partially fry bacon to remove most of the drippings (bacon should still be limp). Drain well and set aside.

Distribute chicken evenly over muffin halves; top each with 1 onion slice and 1 tomato slice. Distribute cheese evenly over each and top each with 2 pieces bacon. Broil about 4 inches from heat until cheese is bubbly and bacon crisp (3 to 5 minutes). Four sandwiches serve 2.

Parmesan Scrambled Egg Sandwiches

⏱ *Preparation time (cooking included): 15 minutes*

That any-time-of-the-day-or-night favorite—scrambled eggs with bacon—takes a turn as a sandwich filling.

Lightly **butter** both sides of 4 slices **whole wheat bread.** Toast both sides of bread in a wide frying pan over medium heat. Remove from pan and keep warm.

Lightly beat together 2 **eggs,** 2 tablespoons *each* chopped **parsley** and freshly cooked or canned **bacon crumbles** (or bacon-flavored vegetable protein chips), ¼ cup grated **Parmesan cheese,** and 2 teaspoons **instant minced onion.** Melt 1 tablespoon **butter** or margarine in pan. Pour egg mixture into pan and stir gently until cooked to your liking. Divide evenly between 2 slices of toasted bread. Top with remaining slices. Makes 2 sandwiches.

Elegant Asparagus Cheese Puffs

⏱ *Preparation time (cooking included): 20 minutes*

There's something special about asparagus. Arranged with ham slices under a blanket of cheese, which puffs up as it's broiled, asparagus brings a touch of class to this sandwich. Serve with soup for a spring brunch or lunch.

> ½ **pound asparagus or 1 can (8 oz.) asparagus spears**
> 2 **slices firm white or wheat bread**
> **Boiling salted water**
> 4 **ounces Swiss cheese, shredded**
> 1 **tablespoon mayonnaise**
> 1½ **teaspoons Dijon mustard**
> ⅛ **teaspoon prepared horseradish**
> 1½ **tablespoons butter or margarine**
> 2 **thin slices cooked ham, 3 to 4 inches square**

Trim asparagus so tip ends fit bread slices; save remaining green ends for other uses. If using fresh asparagus, rinse tips well, then immerse in 1½ inches rapidly boiling salted water in a wide frying pan. Cook, uncovered, just until fork tender (5 to 7 minutes); drain well. If using canned asparagus, heat in its liquid until warm through; drain well.

Combine cheese, mayonnaise, mustard, and horseradish.

Spread butter evenly over both sides of each bread slice. In a wide frying pan over medium heat, toast bread until golden brown on both sides; arrange on a rimmed baking sheet. Top each bread slice with a slice of ham; arrange asparagus evenly on top, then evenly spread cheese mixture over all to completely enclose asparagus.

Broil about 6 inches from heat until cheese mixture browns. Makes 2 sandwiches.

Turkey, Avocado, Bacon Sandwich

⏱ *Preparation time (cooking included): 15 minutes*

Quite a few of your favorite things get together to make this sandwich-and-salad supper. The crowning touch is a velvety dressing of Green Goddess.

For each serving, cook 3 slices **bacon** in a frying pan over medium heat until crisp; drain. Split a large soft **sandwich roll** and toast cut sides, or toast 2 slices firm white bread. Spread with **butter,** margarine, or until liquid evaporates. Add butter and stir until melted, then cook until shallots are soft. Whirl egg yolks in blender, then gradually add butter mixture in a slow, steady stream; sauce will thicken. Chill until ready to use.

Thinly slice beef fillet. Spread each bread slice generously with chilled béarnaise sauce; top with slices of beef, add salt to taste, and cover with remaining bread slices, enclosing beef in béarnaise. Cut each sandwich in 2 or 3 easy-to-handle portions. For picnicking, wrap in plastic wrap and chill until time to serve. Makes 2 sandwiches.

Quick Sloppy Joes

Preparation time (cooking included): 15 minutes

Pickle relish gives a sweet, spicy flavor to this speedy version of an old favorite.

- ¼ teaspoon salt
- ½ pound lean ground beef
- 1 small onion, chopped
  Dash pepper
- ½ can (6-oz. size) tomato paste
- ⅓ cup water
- ¼ cup sweet pickle relish
- 2 hamburger buns, split and toasted

Sprinkle salt in a wide frying pan over medium-high heat; crumble ground beef into pan, add onion, and cook, stirring, until meat is browned and onions are limp (about 5 minutes). Drain and discard any fat. Stir in pepper, tomato paste, water, and pickle relish. Reduce heat and simmer, uncovered, for 1 to 2 minutes or until heated through. Spoon meat mixture over toasted buns. Makes 2 sandwiches.

Marinated Mushroom Sandwiches

Preparation time: 10 minutes. Marinating time: 1 hour

A garden-fresh sandwich pairing mushrooms with Swiss cheese, this one is most easily eaten with a knife and fork.

Stir together 3 tablespoons **olive oil,** 1 tablespoon **lemon juice,** and ¼ teaspoon *each* **garlic salt** and **oregano leaves.** Stir in ¼ pound **mushrooms** (thinly sliced through stem) and ⅓ cup thinly sliced **celery.** Cover and chill, stirring occasionally, for 1 hour or until serving time.

Butter 2 or 4 slices **rye bread.** On each of 2 slices, lay 1 leaf **butter lettuce,** then 1 or 2 slices **Swiss**

mayonnaise. Place side by side on a plate and top evenly with 3 to 4 ounces thinly sliced cooked **turkey** or chicken breast, 2 or 3 thinly sliced **radishes,** the bacon, and several slices of **avocado.** Pile about ½ cup shredded **lettuce** on the side and sprinkle with **green onion** slices. Season with **salt** and **pepper** and garnish with **cherry tomatoes.** Pass **Green Goddess** or blue cheese dressing to serve over. Makes 1 sandwich.

Béarnaise and Beef Fillet Sandwiches

Preparation time (cooking included): 20 minutes

For an elegant picnic or candlelight supper, treat yourselves to thin slices of fillet of beef smothered in béarnaise sauce. Consider creamy mushroom soup (page 4) as a starter, accompanied by champagne.

- ¼ cup red wine vinegar
- ½ cup minced shallots or mild red onion
- ½ teaspoon tarragon
- ½ cup butter or margarine
- 2 egg yolks
- ½ to 1 pound hot or cold cooked beef fillet, trimmed of fat and thinly sliced
- 4 slices firm-textured whole wheat bread or white bread
  Salt

To make béarnaise sauce, simmer wine vinegar, shallots, and tarragon in a small pan over medium heat

cheese. With a slotted spoon, lift mushroom mixture from dressing, let drain briefly, and mound ½ the mixture on each sandwich. Serve open-faced or top each with a slice of bread. Makes 2 sandwiches.

Snap Pizzas

⏱ *Preparation time: 15 minutes*

Big wheels of *knäcker bröd*—the crisp rounds of rye cracker bread from Sweden—form the base of these pizzas. Layer on toppings, slip under the broiler, and they're ready to serve. Just snap into big pieces or cut with a knife to eat out of hand.

If the 11-inch knäcker bröd rounds aren't readily available, use two 7-inch-square seasoned or unseasoned crisp rye crackers in place of one round. (See photograph on facing page.)

Liverwurst and Tybo Pizza

- 1 **round knäcker bröd or two 7-inch-square rye crackers**
- ½ **pound liverwurst, thinly sliced into rings**
- 1 **small mild red onion, thinly sliced lengthwise**
- 6 **to 8 cherry tomatoes, halved**
- ½ **pound tybo cheese, cut into strips (¾ inch wide, 3½ inches long, ¼ inch thick)**
- 1 **jar (4 oz.) marinated mushrooms, drained and sliced**

On knäcker bröd arrange a ring of liverwurst, slightly overlapping. Sprinkle with onion, top with tomatoes, arrange cheese in wheel-spoke fashion, and add mushrooms.

Place on a baking sheet and broil 4 to 6 inches from heat for about 4 minutes or until cheese melts. Serve at once. One pizza serves 2.

Guacamole and Shrimp Pizza

- 1 **large ripe avocado, peeled and pitted**
- 1 **tablespoon lemon or lime juice**
- ¼ **teaspoon *each* ground coriander and garlic powder**
  Few drops liquid hot pepper seasoning
  Salt
- 1 **round knäcker bröd or two 7-inch-square rye crackers**
- ½ **pound small cooked shrimp**
- ⅓ **cup grated Parmesan cheese**

Mash together avocado, lemon juice, coriander, garlic powder, hot pepper seasoning to taste, and salt to taste. Spread evenly over knäcker bröd. Top with

shrimp and sprinkle with Parmesan cheese. Place on a baking sheet and broil 4 to 6 inches from heat for 3 to 4 minutes or until cheese is lightly browned. Serve at once. One pizza serves 2.

Cream Cheese and Smoked Salmon Pizza

- 4 **ounces cream cheese (half an 8-oz. package), at room temperature**
- 1 **teaspoon dill weed**
- 1 **round knäcker bröd or two 7-inch-square rye crackers**
- 1 **or 2 packages (3 oz. *each*) sliced smoked salmon**
- ½ **cup sliced green onion**
- 1 **hard-cooked egg, sliced**

Blend together cream cheese and dill weed. Spread evenly on knäcker bröd. Top with slices of salmon and sprinkle with onion. Broil 4 to 6 inches from heat for 1 minute or until hot. Garnish with egg slices. Serve at once. One pizza serves 2.

Cheese and Green Chile Pizza

- 1 **round knäcker bröd or two 7-inch-square rye crackers**
- 1 **package (6 oz.) sliced provolone or Cheddar cheese**
- 1 **can (4 oz.) diced canned California green chiles, drained**
- 1 **can (about 2¼ oz.) sliced ripe olives, drained**

On knäcker bröd arrange a ring of provolone slices, slightly overlapping. Distribute green chiles over cheese. Top with olives. Place on a baking sheet and broil 4 to 6 inches from heat for about 2 minutes or until cheese melts. Serve at once. One pizza serves 2.

Crunchy Egg Sandwiches

⏱ *Preparation time: 10 minutes*

For a new twist to egg salad sandwiches, try combining bean sprouts and fresh edible-pod peas.

Stir together 2 tablespoons **mayonnaise,** ¼ teaspoon *each* **garlic salt** and **pepper,** and ¾ teaspoon **Dijon mustard.** Add 3 chopped **hard-cooked eggs;** mix to blend.

(Continued on page 24)

PIZZA IS A SNAP when you use rye cracker rounds for the base. Sprinkle on assorted fillings—such as Parmesan-topped shrimp and guacamole (recipe at left)— then broil. To eat, just break into big pieces.

Butter 2 or 4 slices **rye bread,** pumpernickel, or whole wheat bread. On each of 2 slices, lay 1 leaf **butter lettuce** or about ⅓ cup bean sprouts. Arrange 6 to 8 raw **edible-pod peas** (ends and strings removed) over lettuce and mound half the egg salad over each sandwich. Sprinkle each with about 2 teaspoons thinly sliced **green onion,** if desired. Serve open-faced or top with bread. Makes 2 sandwiches.

With a Sandwich Breakfast, You Get a Packaged Meal

Filled with meat and fruit, sandwiches can offer a fine solution to breakfast boredom. Because they make a neatly packaged meal that's quick to assemble and easy to eat, breakfast sandwiches appeal to hurried commuters. At the same time, they're a satisfying and nutritious start to the day.

Here are five sandwich suggestions to spark your creativity. You can vary the meats and fruits to suit individual tastes and to take advantage of leftovers you have on hand— there's no limit to possible combinations.

Smoked Sausage and Apple Sandwich

Split 2 fully cooked **smoked sausage links** lengthwise. Place in a small frying pan over medium heat and brown lightly on all sides, adding a little **butter** or margarine if necessary. Lift out sausage; discard any drippings.

Add to pan about 1 tablespoon **butter** or margarine and about ½ small **apple,** peeled and thinly sliced. Sprinkle lightly with **sugar** and **ground cinnamon.** Cook until apple is golden brown on all sides.

Split, toast, and butter 1 **bagel**. Arrange sausages on one half; top with apple and remaining bagel half. Makes 1 sandwich.

Bacon and Banana Sandwich

In a small frying pan over medium heat, fry 2 to 3 slices **bacon** until crisp; drain well. Toast 2 slices **whole wheat bread** or firm white bread. Spread 1 slice with about 2 tablespoons **chunk-style peanut butter** and arrange bacon over top. Peel 1 small **banana** and slice lengthwise; arrange on bacon. Spread remaining toast with your favorite **fruit jelly** or with butter or margarine and place jelly side down on top of banana slices. Makes 1 sandwich.

Chicken and Orange Sandwich

Toast 2 slices **raisin bread** or firm white bread. Arrange sliced **cooked chicken** or turkey on 1 piece of toast and cover with fresh **orange slices,** canned mandarin oranges (drained), or fresh peach slices. Spread generously with **spiced apple yogurt** or vanilla-flavored yogurt, seasoned to taste with **ground ginger** or chopped crystallized ginger. Top with remaining toast. Makes 1 sandwich.

Ham and Pineapple Sandwich

Generously spread 2 slices **rye bread** with **butter** or margarine. Place 1 to 2 ounces sliced **cooked ham** on unbuttered side of 1 piece of bread. Top with a fresh or canned **pineapple** slice (well drained); sprinkle lightly with **ground nutmeg** and **brown sugar,** then top with 1 to 2 ounces sliced **jack cheese.** Cover with remaining bread slice, unbuttered side down. Cook in a sandwich grill until cheese is melted and bread is toasted. Makes 1 sandwich.

Braunschweiger and Prune Sandwich

Toast 2 slices **raisin bread** or whole wheat bread. Generously spread each slice with **apple butter;** cover 1 slice with 2 to 4 slices (*each* about ¼ inch thick) **braunschweiger** or liverwurst, and arrange halved moist-pack **pitted prunes** or dried apricots on top. Then add **butter lettuce** leaves and remaining toast, apple butter side down. Makes 1 sandwich.

Ground Beef Reuben Sandwiches

Preparation time (cooking included): 15 minutes

Robust is the word for this ground beef version of the Reuben sandwich, which features also the traditional ingredients of Swiss cheese, sauerkraut, and rye bread.

- 1 **can (8-oz. size) sauerkraut**
- ½ **pound lean ground beef**
- ½ **envelope (single-serving size) instant onion soup**
- 1½ **teaspoons prepared mustard**
- ½ **teaspoon Worcestershire**
  Salad oil
- 2 **tablespoons tomato-based chili sauce**
- 2 **sandwich-size slices Swiss cheese**
- 4 **slices Russian rye bread, toasted and buttered**

Turn sauerkraut into a wire strainer, rinse well with water, and drain thoroughly.

Meanwhile, combine ground beef, instant soup, mustard, and Worcestershire; mix well and shape into 2 oval patties, each ½ inch thick.

In a wide frying pan over medium-high heat, cook patties until done to your liking, turning to brown both sides and adding oil if needed. Top each patty with ½ the sauerkraut, drizzle with ½ the chili sauce, and top with 1 slice Swiss cheese. Cover pan and cook just until cheese melts (1 to 2 minutes).

Place each meat patty on a slice of toasted bread; top with another slice of toasted bread. Makes 2 sandwiches.

Monte Cristo Sandwiches

Preparation time (cooking included): 15 minutes

Powdered-sugar-coated Monte Cristo sandwiches are traditionally made with slices of turkey, ham, and Swiss cheese—with currant jelly to spoon over as they are eaten. A beautiful, special treat for brunch.

- 4 **slices white bread**
  Mayonnaise
- 4 **sandwich-size slices Swiss cheese, ⅛ inch thick**
- 2 **slices cooked ham, ⅛ to ¼ inch thick**
- 2 **slices cooked turkey, ⅛ to ¼ inch thick**
- 1 **egg, slightly beaten**
- 2 **tablespoons half-and-half (light cream) or milk**
  Dash salt
- 2 **to 4 tablespoons butter or margarine**
  Powdered sugar
  Parsley
  Currant jelly

Spread one side of each bread slice with a thin coating of mayonnaise. On two of the bread slices, place 2 slices cheese and 1 slice *each* ham and turkey; top with remaining bread slices, mayonnaise side down. Trim crusts and filling to make edges even, if you like. Cut each sandwich in half.

Beat egg with half-and-half and salt, then dip sandwiches into egg mixture. Melt butter in a wide frying pan over medium-high heat; add sandwiches and toast on both sides until cheese melts. Dust with powdered sugar, garnish with parsley, and serve hot with currant jelly to spoon over. Makes 2 sandwiches.

Avocado-Beef Tortilla Pizza

Preparation time (cooking included): 20 minutes

An ingenious way to make a quick pizza is with Mexican flour tortillas. All you do is brush both sides of the tortilla with olive oil, pile on the toppings, and bake in a hot oven. The crusts are thin and chewy-crisp.

- ½ **pound lean ground beef**
- ¼ **teaspoon salt**
- 1 **small clove garlic, minced or pressed**
- ⅛ **pound mushrooms, sliced**
- 2 **tablespoons green chile salsa**
- 2 **large flour tortillas (about 8-inch size)**
  Olive oil or salad oil
- ¼ **cup *each* chopped onion and green pepper**
- 1 **can (2¼ oz.) sliced ripe olives, drained**
- ¼ **pound jack or Mozzarella cheese, shredded**
- ¼ **cup grated Parmesan cheese**
- 1 **small avocado, peeled, pitted, and cut into thin slices**
- ½ **cup sour cream**

Crumble beef into a wide frying pan and stir over medium heat until lightly browned; drain and discard fat. Add salt, garlic, mushrooms, and chile salsa. Cook, stirring, over high heat until liquid has evaporated (about 3 minutes).

Brush tortillas lightly with olive oil on both sides, making sure edges are oiled; place slightly apart on a baking sheet. Spread meat mixture evenly over tortillas; then scatter onion, green pepper, and sliced olives evenly over tops. Sprinkle evenly with jack cheese, then Parmesan.

Bake in a 475° oven until cheese melts and browns slightly (about 7 minutes). Arrange avocado slices over pizza tops. Pass sour cream to spoon over. Makes 2 pizzas or 2 servings.

Quick Quesadillas

⏱ *Preparation time (cooking included): 20 minutes*

Broiled cheese-stuffed *quesadillas* (keh-sah-*thee*-yas) add up to the Mexican equivalent of grilled cheese sandwiches—with flour tortillas taking the place of sliced bread. Combine with a quick green salad and marinated tomatoes.

- ¼ cup *each* shredded Cheddar and jack cheese
- 1 flour tortilla (about 8-inch size)
- 1 slice mild red onion, separated into rings (optional)
- 1 tablespoon chopped, seeded, canned California green chile (optional)
  About 2 teaspoons grated Parmesan cheese (optional)
  About 2 teaspoons butter or margarine, melted

Distribute Cheddar and jack cheese over half the tortilla to within ½ inch of edge; add onion and green chile, if used. Sprinkle with Parmesan, if desired. Fold tortilla over and brush top with melted butter. Turn over onto a baking sheet and brush second side with butter. Broil about 3 inches from heat until top is lightly browned (about 2 minutes). Turn over and broil until other side is browned and cheese is melted (about 2 more minutes). Serve immediately. Makes 1 quesadilla.

Quesadilla variations. To make spicier quesadillas, drizzle 1 tablespoon **taco sauce** over filling.

To substitute a different cheese, pick one that melts easily, such as **Swiss,** American, or teleme.

To make a meat filling, omit either Cheddar or jack; add 1 slice or about ¼ cup diced **cooked chicken,** turkey, ham, or beef.

Pocket Bread Sandwiches

⏱ *Preparation time (cooking included): 20 minutes*

There's no limit to the savory combinations you can stuff into Arab pocket bread (sometimes called peda or pita bread). The flat, chewy rounds, when torn in half, form pockets that are perfect for neatly containing hot or cold sandwich fillings. You can enlarge the

HUMBLE TUNA gets all dressed up for a quick Niçoise supper salad. Combine tuna with both fresh and canned sliced vegetables before tossing with anchovy-flavored dressing (page 15). For variety, stuff salad into pocket bread halves and serve as sandwiches.

pockets by gently working them open with a fork or your fingers.

Spicy Beef and Raisin Filling

- 2 tablespoons slivered almonds
- ½ pound lean ground beef
- ½ small onion, chopped
- ¼ cup *each* tomato-based chili sauce and water
- 2 tablespoons raisins
- ⅛ teaspoon ground cinnamon
  Dash ground cumin
  Salt and pepper
- 2 Arab pocket breads, cut in half
- ½ cup shredded jack cheese
- 1 cup shredded iceberg lettuce
- 6 to 8 cherry tomatoes, halved

Spread almonds in a shallow pan and toast in a 350° oven for 8 to 10 minutes or until golden; set aside.

In a wide frying pan over medium-high heat, crumble in beef and cook until browned, stirring often. Add onion and cook until limp. Drain and discard fat. Mix in chili sauce, water, raisins, cinnamon, cumin, and salt and pepper to taste. Cook, uncovered, stirring often, until liquid has evaporated (about 5 minutes). Stir in almonds.

Spoon hot meat mixture into pocket bread halves and top evenly with cheese, lettuce, and tomato halves. Makes 2 sandwiches.

Middle Eastern Lamb Patty Filling

- ½ pound lean ground lamb
- ½ teaspoon ground cumin
- ¼ cup chopped onion
- ¼ teaspoon salt
- 1 egg
- 1 tablespoon fine dry bread crumbs
  Salad oil
- 2 Arab pocket breads, cut in half
  Tender inner romaine leaves
- 6 to 8 cherry tomatoes, halved
- ½ mild red onion, thinly sliced
- ½ cup unflavored yogurt

Mix together lamb, cumin, onion, salt, egg, and bread crumbs. Shape into balls, using 1½ tablespoons for each; then flatten balls into ½-inch-thick patties.

In a wide frying pan over medium-high heat, brown lamb patties on both sides, without crowding, until all are done to your liking. Add oil, if needed.

Evenly fill each pocket bread half with meat patties, romaine leaves, tomato halves, and onion slices. Pass yogurt to spoon into each sandwich. Makes 2 sandwiches.

MEATS

What could be easier than meat for two? Two steaks, two chops, two hamburgers ...simple! Not to mention boring!

Happily, you don't have to choose between that kind of repetition and the other kind—the kind that comes with endless leftovers. There is a good middle ground, and it's covered on the following pages, with rack of lamb and prime rib for two, pot roasts and other meats that have big taste but are small enough for two, stews in manageable quantities that cook in reasonable time, ethnic dishes such as moussaka and schnitzel, and meltingly good special-occasion meats like pork tenderloin with onion-apple cream. Beef, liver, veal, pork, lamb—they're all here. Of course there will be many times when you'll want to take the two-chops route, but it doesn't have to be a way of life.

Our recipes list quantities of meat to buy, but as a further help, we suggest the following:

Waste-free meats are good selections for two—boneless veal and ham, ground meats, liver, and stew meat are all excellent choices; plan on ½ to ¾ pound for two servings. When buying meats with some bone—steaks or roasts, for example—allow about 1¼ pounds for two. And with very bony cuts such as lamb or beef shanks, spareribs, or shortribs, you'll need about 2 pounds.

Prime Rib for Two

Preparation time: 5 minutes. Freeze meat ahead. Cooking time: 1 hour and 15 minutes

A one-rib roast is the perfect size for two servings. First, freeze the roast. Then it goes straight to the oven, where the outside sears before the inside thaws, deliciously capturing meat juices. Two big potatoes do "book end" duty in the oven, then help round out the meal, which might well end with chocolate ice cream laced with Grand Marnier.

- 1 rib of a standing rib roast (about 2½ lb.)
- 1 tablespoon salad oil or olive oil
- 1 small clove garlic, minced or pressed
- 2 large baking potatoes

Wrap meat well and freeze until solid.

Combine oil and garlic; rub evenly over frozen meat. Stand roast, rib bone down, on a rimmed baking sheet or broiler pan between the 2 potatoes, placed like book ends. *Roast frozen; do not thaw.*

Roast, uncovered, in a 400° oven for 1 hour and 15 minutes for rare meat, 1 hour and 25 minutes for medium rare, 1 hour and 35 to 40 minutes for well done. If you wish, insert a meat thermometer through fat layer into center of roast, not touching bone, after it has cooked for about 1 hour, and continue cooking until meat is done to your liking (130° to 135° for rare). Let stand for about 5 minutes before carving.

Beef Shank Pot Roast

Preparation time: 10 minutes. Cooking time: 2 hours and 15 minutes

Choose a casserole with a tight-fitting lid for this midget pot roast. You might round out the menu with hot rolls and a fruit salad that doubles as dessert.

- 2 meaty slices beef shank, cut 1½ inches thick (about 1½ lb.)
- 1 tablespoon all-purpose flour
- 2 single-serving-size packages instant onion soup
- 1 clove garlic, minced or pressed
- ½ cup dry red wine
- 1 cup water
- 1 teaspoon Worcestershire
- ¼ teaspoon thyme leaves
- 6 small white boiling onions
- 3 medium-size carrots, cut in about 1½-inch pieces

Sprinkle meat with flour, shake off excess, and place in a 1½ to 2-quart casserole. Sprinkle evenly with onion soup mix and add garlic, wine, water, Worcestershire, and thyme. Cover tightly and bake in a 375°

oven for 1 hour. Remove from oven, turn meat over, and add onions and carrots, tucking them in around meat. Cover and continue baking for about 1 hour and 15 minutes or until meat and vegetables are tender. Skim any excess fat from broth.

One-person pot roast. Use 1 slice **beef shank** (about 12 oz.) cut 1½ inches thick; enough **flour** to coat lightly; 1 single-serving-size package **onion soup mix;** 1 small clove **garlic,** minced or pressed; ¼ cup **dry red wine;** ½ cup **water;** ½ teaspoon **Worcestershire;** ⅛ teaspoon **thyme leaves;** 3 small white **boiling onions;** and 2 small **carrots,** cut in 1½-inch pieces. Bake in a 1-quart covered casserole.

Beef with Chinese Cabbage

🕐 *Preparation time (cooking included): 30 minutes*

Here is a colorful one-dish meal that uses lots of greens and is sparing of calories. Stir-fry it in a wok or a wide frying pan. Before starting to cook, be sure to have all the ingredients prepared—and that includes the cooking sauce.

- ½ to ¾ **pound lean boneless beef (such as sirloin, top round, flank)**
- 1 **teaspoon cornstarch**
- 1 **tablespoon soy sauce**
- ½ **teaspoon minced or grated fresh ginger, or** ¼ **teaspoon ground ginger**
- ½ **small head celery cabbage (also called Chinese cabbage) or regular cabbage**
- 4 **tablespoons salad oil**
- 1 **clove garlic, minced or pressed**
- 1 **medium-size red or green bell pepper, seeded and cut in 1-inch squares**
  Cooking sauce (recipe follows)
- 2 **green onions, thinly sliced**

Trim off and discard excess fat from meat; cut meat in ⅛-inch-thick diagonal slices. Blend cornstarch and soy with ginger in a bowl; mix in meat and set aside.

Cut celery cabbage across in ¾-inch slices (or regular cabbage in ¾-inch wedges).

In a wide frying pan or wok over high heat, heat 2 tablespoons of the oil; add meat mixture. Stir and turn until browned (2 to 3 minutes); turn out into serving dish.

Reheat pan; add remaining 2 tablespoons oil. When oil is hot, put in garlic and green pepper; stir and cook for about 30 seconds. Add cabbage and continue to stir and cook for about 2 minutes or until cabbage is tender-crisp and bright green.

Return meat to pan, add cooking sauce, and cook, stirring, until mixture boils and thickens (about 2 minutes). Stir in green onions, then turn out into serving dish.

Cooking sauce. Mix together 1 tablespoon *each* **cornstarch** and **sugar** with ½ cup regular-strength **beef broth,** 1 tablespoon **soy sauce** or oyster sauce, and 1 tablespoon **dry sherry** or white wine.

Paprika Pot Roast

🕐 *Preparation time: 20 minutes. Cooking time: 2 hours and 15 minutes*

When you have some time to let a dish simmer away, try Hungarian-inspired pot roast. It takes a little over 2 hours and comes out melt-in-your-mouth tender. Serve accompaniments of sour cream and noodles.

- 2 **tablespoons butter or margarine**
- 1½ **pound bone-in beef chuck roast**
- 2 **small onions, sliced**
- 1 **teaspoon caraway seed**
- 1½ **teaspoons paprika**
- ¾ **teaspoon salt**
  Dash pepper
- ¾ **cup water**
- 1 **tablespoon all-purpose flour**
- ½ **cup sour cream**
  Hot cooked noodles

Melt butter in a frying pan over medium heat; add roast and brown on all sides; remove meat to platter. Add onions to pan and cook, stirring occasionally, over medium heat, until limp; then stir in caraway seed, paprika, salt, pepper, and water. Return roast to pan, cover, and reduce heat to low; cook until meat is fork tender (about 2 hours and 15 minutes).

Remove roast to a platter and keep warm. Skim off

and discard excess fat from pan juices. In a bowl, gradually stir ⅓ cup of the juices into flour until smooth; blend in sour cream. Stir this mixture back into juices in pan and cook until thickened; pour into serving bowl. Serve pot roast with noodles; pass sauce to spoon over servings.

Beef Stroganoff

🕐 *Preparation time (cooking included): 20 minutes*

Quickly browned strips of beef blended with mushrooms and sour cream can be served over hot noodles or rice in minutes.

1 **pound beef chuck steak or roast**
2 **to 3 tablespoons butter or margarine**
1 **tablespoon salad oil**
¼ **pound mushrooms, sliced**
¼ **cup finely chopped onion**
½ **teaspoon *each* salt and Worcestershire**
  Dash *each* paprika and pepper
½ **cup sour cream**
  Chopped parsley
  Hot cooked noodles or rice

Cut out and discard bone and fat; cut meat into thin bite-size strips. Heat 2 tablespoons of the butter with oil in a wide frying pan over medium-high heat until foamy. Add mushrooms and onion and cook, stirring, until golden; lift out and set aside.

Add remaining 1 tablespoon butter to pan. Add beef strips and cook over high heat, turning meat and shaking pan, just until browned. Remove pan from heat; stir in reserved mushroom-onion mixture, salt, Worcestershire, paprika, pepper, and sour cream. Return pan to low heat and cook, stirring constantly, just until sauce is heated through—do not boil. Sprinkle with parsley. Serve over noodles.

Sesame Steak

🕐 *Preparation time (cooking included): 20 minutes*

Toasted sesame seed butter enhances thick, tender steak, and it's also good spooned over baked or new potatoes cooked in their jackets. Serve with sliced tomatoes, a green vegetable, and your favorite tart fruit sherbet.

1 **large porterhouse steak, cut 1 inch thick, or other tender steak of your choice**
  Salt and pepper
2 **teaspoons sesame seed**
¼ **cup butter or margarine**
1 **clove garlic, minced or pressed**

Slash at 1 to 2-inch intervals through outside layer of fat on steak just to, but not into, meat. Season steak with salt and pepper to taste and place on a rack in a broiler pan about 2 inches from heat. Broil until done to your liking (about 6 minutes per side for rare).

As steak cooks, toast sesame seeds by shaking them in a small pan over medium-high heat. When they are richly browned, add butter and garlic. When butter melts, remove from heat and let stand until steak is done.

Transfer meat to a serving platter and pour butter sauce over it. Serve immediately, cutting thin slanting slices across grain of meat. Spoon some of the sesame butter over each serving.

Sesame steak for one. Substitute a 6 to 8-ounce **boneless tender beef steak** from the rib or loin, cut 1 inch thick. Use 1 teaspoon **sesame seed**, 2 tablespoons **butter** or margarine, and 1 small clove **garlic.**

Steak and Onions, Austrian-style

🕐 *Preparation time (cooking included): 50 minutes*

Plenty of onions, cooked slowly to sweetness, are an unbeatable addition to quickly cooked steak. Accompany with gingered carrots, spinach-stuffed mushrooms (page 64), and for dessert, flaky apple turnovers from the freezer. (See photograph on facing page.)

1 **tablespoon butter or margarine**
1 **tablespoon salad oil**
2 **large onions, thinly sliced and separated into rings**
1 **small clove garlic, minced or pressed**
2 **beef fillets or ¾ to 1 pound top sirloin steak (¾ inch thick), cut into 2 equal pieces**
  Salt and pepper
¼ **cup dry vermouth or regular-strength beef broth**
  Chopped parsley (optional)

Heat butter and oil in a wide frying pan over medium-low heat. Add onion and garlic and cook, stirring occasionally, until onion is limp and golden (about 30 minutes). Increase heat to brown onion slightly; remove from pan.

(Continued on page 32)

SLOWLY SAUTÉED ONION RINGS crown pan-fried steaks, Austrian-style (recipe above). Spinach soufflé-stuffed mushroom caps (page 65) and gingered sesame carrots (page 64) make colorful and tasty side dishes.

Meanwhile, sprinkle steaks with salt and pepper. In same pan, over high heat, brown steak quickly on both sides adding a little more butter and oil, if needed; cook until meat is done to your liking (about 2½ minutes on each side for rare). Remove to a warm platter.

Add vermouth to pan; heat quickly to reduce liquid slightly, stirring up browned bits from pan. Reduce heat, stir in onion, and heat thoroughly. Spoon onion mixture over steak. Sprinkle with parsley, if desired.

Hawaiian Short Ribs

🕐 *Preparation time: 10 minutes. Cooking time: 2 hours*

White or brown rice complements these baked short ribs with their sesame seed sauce. Add a green vegetable or crisp salad, and lime-drizzled papaya halves for dessert.

- 1½ **tablespoons sesame seed**
  About 2 pounds beef short ribs, cut in 2 to 3-inch lengths
- 1 **small onion, sliced**
- ¾ **cup water**
- ¼ **cup soy sauce**
- 2 **tablespoons packed brown sugar**
- 1 **small clove garlic, minced or pressed**
- ⅛ **teaspoon *each* ground ginger and pepper**
- 1 **small dried hot chile pepper, seeded and crushed**
- 1 **teaspoon *each* cornstarch and water**

In a 2 to 3-quart ovenproof pan, toast sesame seed over medium heat until lightly browned, shaking pan often to toast evenly. Remove from heat and arrange ribs and onion on top of seeds.

Combine water, soy, brown sugar, garlic, ginger, pepper, and chile pepper; pour over meat. Cover and bake in a 400° oven for 2 hours or until meat is fork tender; stir well occasionally.

Lift meat to a warm serving dish; keep warm. Skim fat from pan juices. Combine cornstarch and water, stir into juices, and cook, stirring, until thickened; pour over meat.

winner even with those who usually say no thanks to liver. Consider serving carrots with sesame seed (page 64) and a salad of grapefruit and avocado slices with oil and vinegar dressing.

- ¾ **pound liver, cut in ½-inch-thick slices**
  Salt, pepper, and all-purpose flour
- 1 **egg, slightly beaten**
- ⅓ **cup saltine cracker crumbs**
- ¼ **cup butter or margarine**
- 2 **tablespoons lemon juice**
- ½ **teaspoon sugar**

Sprinkle liver slices with salt and pepper, then coat lightly with flour; shake off excess. Dip each floured liver slice into beaten egg, then into cracker crumbs until evenly coated. Melt 2 tablespoons of the butter in a wide frying pan over medium-high heat. Cook liver slices quickly until nicely browned on both sides and juicy-pink inside (about 3 to 4 minutes total).

Remove liver to a serving plate and keep warm. Melt remaining 2 tablespoons butter in pan, add lemon juice and sugar, and stir until sugar is dissolved. Pour sauce over liver and serve.

Liver in Lemon Butter

🕐 *Preparation time (cooking included): 20 minutes*

Liver is an economical choice for a main dish for two. Cooked briefly to keep the meat juicy and pink inside, then served with a sprightly lemon butter, this dish is a

Liver Provençale

🕐 *Preparation time (cooking included): 15 minutes*

Garlic and herbs flavor another quick-cooking liver entrée. Accompany it with buttered green beans and a robust salad with an oil and vinegar dressing.

½ to ¾ pound top round steak
¼ cup *each* salad oil and chopped onion
2 tablespoons white wine vinegar
¼ teaspoon *each* salt and oregano leaves, crumbled
Dash pepper
2 tablespoons butter or margarine
¼ pound sliced mushrooms
½ cup halved cherry tomatoes
2 green onions, sliced (include some green tops)

Place steak in a shallow baking dish. Mix together oil, onion, vinegar, salt, oregano, and pepper; pour over steak. Cover and refrigerate for several hours, turning meat occasionally.

Melt butter in a wide frying pan over medium heat. Add mushrooms and cook until liquid evaporates; keep warm.

Remove steak from marinade, drain briefly, and place on rack in broiler pan or on a grill about 4 inches from heat. Cook for about 4 minutes on each side for rare to medium-rare, basting often with marinade.

To serve, top steak with mushrooms. Slice meat in thin diagonal slices across the grain. Garnish with tomatoes and green onion slices.

¾ pound liver, cut in ½-inch-thick slices
Salt, pepper, and all-purpose flour
1 tablespoon butter or margarine
1 tablespoon salad oil
1 large clove garlic, minced or pressed
⅛ teaspoon dry rosemary, crumbled
¼ cup regular-strength beef broth
Chopped parsley

Cut each slice of liver in ½ to 1-inch-wide cross-grain strips. Sprinkle with salt and pepper, then coat with flour, shaking off excess. Heat butter and oil in a wide frying pan over medium-high heat. Add garlic and liver. Brown liver well on 1 side (about 2½ minutes), then turn and sprinkle with rosemary. Continue cooking for about 2½ minutes longer or until browned but still slightly pink inside when slashed. Remove liver to a warm serving dish.

Add broth to pan and cook, stirring up browned bits, until liquid is reduced by about half. Pour over liver. Sprinkle with parsley.

Top Round with Mushrooms

⏱ *Preparation time: 20 minutes. Marinating time: 2 hours*

Slowly marinated, then quickly broiled or grilled, round steak becomes as tender and full of flavor as a more expensive cut of beef. Mushrooms, cherry tomatoes, and green onions are the crowning touch.

Ground Beef Burgundy

⏱ *Preparation time (cooking included): 15 minutes*

Ground beef takes the place of beef chunks in this variation of the traditional French boeuf bourguignon. It goes together quickly with supplies from your kitchen shelf.

½ pound lean ground beef
1½ teapoons all-purpose flour
½ cup dry red wine
1 tablespoon instant minced onion
1 can (2 oz.) sliced mushrooms, drained
¼ teaspoon thyme leaves
¼ bay leaf
1 clove garlic, minced or pressed
1 tablespoon chopped parsley
Hot cooked rice or noodles

In a wide frying pan over medium-high heat, cook beef until crumbly. Stir in flour and cook until it browns slightly. Add wine, instant onion, mushrooms, thyme, bay leaf, and garlic. Simmer, uncovered, stirring occasionally, for about 5 minutes or until liquid is slightly reduced. Remove bay leaf and turn meat mixture into a serving dish; sprinkle with chopped parsley. Serve over rice or noodles.

Beef and Avocado Loaves

⏱ *Preparation time: 15 minutes. Cooking time: 15 minutes*

Avocado and cheese are the surprise stuffing in these plump individual meat loaves. Tortilla chips, sliced tomatoes, and beer or dry red wine round out the meal nicely.

- ¾ pound lean ground beef
- 3 tablespoons fine dry bread crumbs
- ½ cup tomato-based chili sauce
- 1 egg
- ¼ cup finely chopped onion
- ½ teaspoon salt
- ⅛ teaspoon pepper
- 1½ teaspoons Worcestershire
- ½ cup shredded jack cheese
- 2 tablespoons seeded and diced canned California green chiles
- 1 small avocado, peeled, pitted, and halved

Mix together ground beef, bread crumbs, ¼ cup of the chili sauce, egg, onion, salt, pepper, and Worcestershire. Divide mixture into 4 equal portions and flatten each into an oval patty about 5 inches long. Combine cheese and 1 tablespoon of the green chiles; stuff evenly into avocado halves and place each, cheese side down, on a beef patty. Top with remaining patties and pinch together to enclose avocado. Place, flat side down, on a rimmed baking sheet.

Bake in a 375° oven for 15 minutes or until meat is barely pink when slashed. Meanwhile, combine remaining ¼ cup chili sauce with remaining 1 tablespoon green chiles; heat. Pass in a bowl to spoon over meat.

Mushroom-Raisin Meat Loaf

⏱ *Preparation time: 5 minutes. Cooking time: 1 hour*

Here's a loaf that can pass for a French terrine. Serve hot for dinner, or chill it and take it on a picnic to slice and serve on firm-textured bread. Bacon slices decorate the top and add flavor to the spicy meat mixture. (See photograph on facing page.)

AN ELEGANT PICNIC: slices of mushroom-raisin meat loaf (recipe above); mugs of chilled, makeahead curried broccoli soup (page 4); marinated mushroom salad sprinkled with chunks of zesty blue cheese (page 14); and fresh raspberries and cream cheese to spread on firm ginger cookies.

- ½ cup fine dry bread crumbs
- ¾ pound lean ground beef
- ¼ pound bulk sausage
- 1 egg
- 1 tablespoon nonfat dry milk
- 2 tablespoons raisins
- ¼ pound mushrooms, coarsely chopped
- 1 tablespoon Worcestershire
- ¼ teaspoon *each* salt and pepper
- 2 strips bacon, cut in half
- 2 tablespoons catsup

Mix together crumbs, ground beef, sausage, egg, dry milk, raisins, mushrooms, Worcestershire, salt, and pepper. Press lightly into a 1-quart baking dish, tureen, or loaf pan. Lay bacon strips lengthwise on loaf and drizzle with catsup. Bake, uncovered, in a 350° oven for 1 hour or until meat is no longer pink inside when slashed.

Flaming Veal Amandine

⏱ *Preparation time (cooking included): 20 minutes*

What could be more elegant and delicious than veal flamed in Marsala wine and bathed in an almond cream sauce? If time is of the essence, you can partially prepare the dish ahead, then finish it in minutes.

- ¾ pound boneless veal, cut about ½ inch thick
- 2 tablespoons butter or margarine
- ½ cup sliced or slivered almonds
  Salt
- 3 tablespoons Marsala wine or brandy
- 1 tablespoon lemon juice
- ⅓ cup whipping cream

Trim off and discard membrane from veal. Place meat between 2 sheets of wax paper and pound ¼ inch thick with smooth side of a mallet.

In a wide frying pan over medium heat, melt 1 tablespoon of the butter. Add almonds; cook, stirring, until golden; spoon nuts out of pan and set aside. Melt 1 more tablespoon of the butter over high heat. Sprinkle meat lightly with salt and cook, without crowding, until meat is lightly browned on each side. Set meat aside as it cooks; add more butter to frying pan, if needed.

When all meat is cooked, return it and any juices to frying pan. Add Marsala and set aflame at once (*not under an exhaust fan or flammable items*), shaking pan until flames subside. Pour lemon juice over meat, then lift meat from pan and arrange in a serving dish; keep warm. (If cooked ahead, place pieces of meat side-by-side in a shallow rimmed pan, cover, and chill. To reheat, uncover and place in a 375° oven for 3 to 4 minutes while preparing sauce.)

(Continued on next page)

Pour cream into frying pan. Boil rapidly, stirring, until large shiny bubbles form over entire surface and cream is a rich golden color; drain any juices from meat into sauce. Stir in almonds and spoon sauce over meat; serve at once.

Veal Piccata

🕐 *Preparation time (cooking included): 20 minutes*

For a last-minute dinner that's out of the ordinary, cook lemony veal piccata strips and serve with buttered broccoli spears.

- ¾ **pound boneless veal, cut ½ inch thick**
- 1 **tablespoon all-purpose flour**
- ½ **teaspoon salt**
- ⅛ **teaspoon pepper**
- 3 **tablespoons butter or margarine**
- ⅓ **cup dry white wine**
- 1 **teaspoon grated lemon peel**
  Lemon slices

Place meat between 2 sheets of wax paper and pound ¼ inch thick with smooth side of a mallet. Cut meat into strips about 1½ inches wide and 3 inches long. Mix together flour, salt, and pepper. Lightly dust meat with flour mixture, shaking off excess.

Melt 2 tablespoons of the butter in a wide frying pan over medium-high heat. Add meat and cook quickly, turning to brown both sides (takes about 4 minutes total).

Remove meat to a warm platter. To pan, add wine and bring to a boil, scraping up browned bits. Stir in lemon peel and remaining 1 tablespoon butter; heat until melted. Spoon sauce over veal and garnish with lemon slices.

Veal piccata for one. Pound 6 to 8 ounces **veal cutlet** as directed above. Sprinkle with **salt** and **pepper** and enough **all-purpose flour** to coat lightly; shake off excess. Cook in 1 tablespoon **butter** or margarine. For sauce, use 3 tablespoons **dry white wine**, ½ teaspoon **lemon peel**, and 1½ teaspoons **butter** or margarine. Garnish with 2 thin **lemon** slices.

Veal Stew with Spring Vegetables

🕐 *Preparation time: 20 minutes. Cooking time: 1 hour and 30 minutes*

This stew resembles the delicate French *blanquette de veau* or white veal stew—white because of the cream sauce it's served in. If you make it ahead, wait until you reheat it to add the egg yolk.

- 1½ **tablespoons butter or margarine**
- 1 **medium-size onion, finely chopped**
- 1 **small carrot, finely chopped**
- 1 **pound boneless veal stew meat, cut in 1-inch cubes**
- ¾ **cup water**
- ⅛ **teaspoon thyme leaves**
- ½ **bay leaf**
- ½ **teaspoon salt**
- ¼ **pound small whole mushrooms**
- ¾ **cup frozen peas, thawed**
- ⅓ **cup whipping cream**
- ½ **teaspoon cornstarch**
- 1 **egg yolk**

Melt butter in a wide frying pan over medium heat; add onion and carrot and cook, uncovered, just until vegetables are soft but not browned, stirring occasionally. Add veal and cook, covered, over medium-low heat, stirring occasionally, until meat loses pink color and releases juices. Add water, thyme, bay leaf, and salt; simmer, covered, for about 1½ hours or until meat is very tender when pierced.

With a slotted spoon, lift meat from juices and set aside. Discard bay leaf. Bring liquid to boiling and add mushrooms; cook rapidly, uncovered, for 5 minutes; then add peas and cook for 2 minutes more. Blend cream with cornstarch and add to boiling liquid, stirring until slightly thickened. Return meat to pan and heat through. Remove pan from heat. Stir a little of the hot liquid into egg yolk, then return to pan, stirring to blend. Serve in large soup bowls.

Schnitzel

🕐 *Preparation time (cooking included): 30 minutes*

Golden veal cutlets and mushrooms topped with a sour cream wine sauce—that's what makes up this version of an Austrian classic.

- ½ **pound boneless veal, cut in ½-inch-thick slices**
- ½ **cup fine dry bread crumbs**
- ½ **teaspoon salt**
- ¼ **teaspoon pepper**
  About 3 tablespoons all-purpose flour
- 1 **egg beaten with 1 tablespoon milk**
- 5 **tablespoons butter or margarine**
- ¼ **pound mushrooms, sliced**
- 2 **tablespoons finely chopped onion**
- ½ **cup *each* dry white wine and regular-strength chicken broth**
- 2 **teaspoons paprika**
- ½ **cup sour cream**

Place meat between 2 sheets of wax paper and pound ¼ inch thick with smooth side of a mallet.

Combine bread crumbs, salt, and pepper. Dust cutlets with about 2 tablespoons of the flour, shake off excess, dip them into egg mixture, then into crumb mixture. In a wide frying pan, melt 4 tablespoons of the butter over medium heat and cook cutlets until golden (2 to 3 minutes on each side). Place on a platter and keep warm.

Add remaining 1 tablespoon butter to pan and cook mushrooms and onion until onion is limp. Add wine, broth, and paprika; bring to a rolling boil, scraping up browned bits from pan. Stir remaining 1 tablespoon flour into sour cream, then stir into broth mixture and cook until hot through and slightly thickened. Pour over cutlets and serve at once.

Veal Strips Sauté with Artichokes

🕐 *Preparation time (cooking included): 15 minutes*

For a little taste of Italy, accompany this quick sauté with green noodles and an antipasto-style salad of thinly sliced tomatoes, olives, and anchovies.

- ¾ **pound boneless veal, cut in ½-inch-thick slices**
- 2 **tablespoons all-purpose flour**
- ¼ **teaspoon salt**
- ⅛ **teaspoon *each* pepper and paprika**
- 1 **jar (6 oz.) marinated artichoke hearts, drained**
- 1 **medium-size onion, sliced**
  Butter or margarine
- ¼ **cup water or regular-strength chicken broth**
- 1 **tablespoon lemon juice**
- ½ **cup sour cream**
- 2 **tablespoons grated Parmesan cheese**
  Hot cooked green noodles

Trim all membrane from veal slices; place meat between 2 sheets of wax paper and pound ¼ inch thick with smooth side of a mallet. Cut each piece into ¾-inch-wide strips. Combine flour, salt, pepper, and paprika. Dredge meat in flour mixture, shaking off excess.

Drain artichoke marinade into a wide frying pan (reserve artichokes for garnish); cook over medium heat until bubbly. Add meat strips, a few at a time, and cook quickly, stirring, until well browned (3 to 5 minutes); lift out and set aside.

When all the meat is browned, add onion to pan with butter, if needed; cook onion until limp (about 5 minutes). Add water and stir to loosen browned bits. Stir in lemon juice, sour cream, cheese, and veal strips. Heat through (do not boil) and serve over noodles. Garnish with artichoke hearts.

Lamb, Persian-style

🕐 *Preparation time: 20 minutes. Cooking time: 1 hour and 10 minutes*

A tantalizing combination of subtly spiced lamb and fresh nectarine slices, this dish is enhanced by plain yogurt—you spoon it over both meat and fruit. Brown or white rice goes well with this. The meat cooks while you read the evening paper.

- 2 **teaspoons salad oil**
- ⅓ **cup chopped onion**
- ¼ **teaspoon salt**
  Dash pepper
- ½ **teaspoon *each* ground cinnamon and cloves**
- 2 **teaspoons sugar**
- ¾ **to 1 pound lean boneless lamb shoulder, cut in bite-size pieces**
- 1 **tablespoon lemon juice**
  About 2 tablespoons water
- 1 **large nectarine or peach**
- 1 **tablespoon butter or margarine**

Heat oil in a wide frying pan over medium-high heat. Add onion and cook, stirring, until limp. Then stir in salt, pepper, cinnamon, cloves, and sugar. Add meat, turning to coat with onion mixture. Add lemon juice and 1 tablespoon of the water; cover and simmer for about 1 hour and 10 minutes or until meat is fork tender. Stir occasionally during cooking, adding a little more water if needed. Discard any fat and turn meat into a serving dish.

Meanwhile, cut nectarine or peeled peach into thick slices. Heat butter in a small frying pan over medium heat. Put in fruit and cook, turning gently, just until heated through (about 3 minutes). Arrange on top of meat.

Lamb Kebabs

⏱ *Preparation time: 15 minutes. Marinating time: 4 hours. Heat coals: 35 minutes. Cooking time: 20 minutes*

A tart lemon marinade accents these lamb kebabs—you'll want to plan ahead for overnight marinating. They're good with rice pilaf, stuffed eggplant (page 65), and well-chilled melon. (See photograph on facing page.)

    ¾ to 1 pound tender boneless lamb, cut in 1½ to
        2-inch cubes
        Lemon marinade (recipe follows)
    1 small red or green bell pepper
    1 small onion
    2 lemon slices
    4 medium-size mushrooms

Combine meat and marinade; cover and chill for 4 hours or until next day. Seed pepper and cut into 1½-inch squares. Cut onion into 2 wedges and separate each into layers.

Remove meat from marinade and drain; reserve marinade for basting. Thread a 10 to 12-inch skewer with a mushroom and a pepper; then alternate meat and pepper, using ½ of each. Add lemon slice and another pepper and mushroom. Repeat on second skewer.

To barbecue, place skewers on a grill about 6 inches above a bed of low-glowing coals and cook, turning and basting with marinade, for about 20 minutes, until meat is browned on all sides and still slightly pink inside (cut a gash to test).

Lemon marinade. Combine 2 tablespoons chopped **parsley**, ⅓ cup **salad oil**, 1 tablespoon **soy sauce**, ½ teaspoon *each* **dry mustard** and **Worcestershire**, ¼ cup **lemon juice,** and 1 clove **garlic,** minced or pressed.

Spicy Barbecued Lamb Chops

⏱ *Preparation time: 10 minutes. Marinating time: 4 hours. Heat coals: 35 minutes. Cooking time: 15 minutes*

Lamb chops marinate in a spicy concoction overnight, for barbecuing the next day. Another time, try this versatile marinade recipe for chicken.

    ⅔ cup dry red wine
    2 tablespoons olive oil or salad oil
    2 cloves garlic, minced or pressed
    ½ teaspoon each salt and ground cumin
    ¼ teaspoon ground cinnamon
    2 teaspoons cumin seed
    ¼ cup finely chopped onion
    2 shoulder lamb chops, cut about ¾ inch thick

In a shallow baking pan, stir together wine, oil, garlic, salt, ground cumin, cinnamon, cumin seed, and onion. Turn lamb chops in marinade to moisten all sides, then arrange in a single layer. Cover and refrigerate for at least 4 hours or until next day, turning chops over in marinade occasionally, if possible.

To barbecue, remove chops from marinade and drain; reserve marinade. Place chops on a grill about 6 inches above a bed of hot-glowing coals. Cook, turning occasionally and basting often with marinade, until meat is done to your liking (about 15 minutes total for medium-well).

Grilled Lamb Steaks

⏱ *Preparation time: 15 minutes. Marinating time: 4 hours. Heat coals: 35 minutes. Cooking time: 12 minutes*

For this dish, the longer the lamb marinates, the better the flavor—plan on 6 hours, at least. The best way is to marinate it overnight for barbecuing the next day. Fresh broccoli spears laced with butter are a good accompaniment.

    2 lamb leg steaks (about 1 lb.), cut about ¾ inch
        thick
    ½ cup cold strong coffee
    ¼ cup firmly packed brown sugar
    1 tablespoon prepared mustard
    ½ teaspoon Worcestershire
    2 tablespoons lemon juice
        Dash liquid hot pepper seasoning
    1 clove garlic, minced or pressed

Place steaks in a single layer in a shallow baking pan. Combine coffee, sugar, mustard, Worcestershire, lemon juice, hot pepper seasoning, and garlic; mix well and pour over lamb. Cover and chill for 4 hours or until next day. Turn steaks several times, if possible.

To barbecue, remove steaks from marinade and drain; reserve marinade. Place steaks on a grill about 4 inches above a bed of hot-glowing coals. Grill, basting often with marinade, until nicely browned on both sides (about 12 minutes total for medium-well).

IN THIS MIDDLE-EASTERN inspired barbecue, kebabs of lamb chunks, whole mushrooms, and thick slices of tomato, pepper, and lemon (recipe above) cook on a grill. Accompany entrée with stuffed eggplant halves (page 65), Armenian cracker bread, tall glasses of apricot nectar, and fruit and baklava for dessert.

Three Ways to Use Leg of Lamb

When you cook for just two, a whole leg of lamb—though certainly appealing—may seem a bit unwieldy. But with the help of your butcher, the leg can be divided into easily handled portions that you can use for three different mouth-watering entrées.

After selecting a full-cut leg of lamb, ask the meat cutter to first saw off four slices, each about an inch thick, from the large end (sirloin section). This gives you two hip blocks for a quickly assembled lamb chop *cassoulet*, and two leg steaks to pan-broil.

Then have him bone the remainder of the leg, cutting off the small shank end (about 1 lb.) for use in lemon-accented braised lamb stew. The center cut can be rolled and tied for an oven roast, which will give you a hearty dinner with plenty of cooked meat left over—use it for curried lamb another night; there may still be enough left for lamb sandwiches.

Generally, meat market personnel will do the cutting and boning without charge while you wait; some may require a day or two of notice. Once you have the meat home, cook the dishes in any order you choose; wrap and freeze the remaining cuts until needed.

Lamb Chop Cassoulet

Cut 2 strips **bacon** into 1-inch pieces; cook in a small frying pan over medium heat until lightly browned. Pour off all but about 2 tablespoons of the drippings and add 1 medium-size **onion,** sliced, and 1 clove **garlic,** minced or pressed; cook until onion is limp.

In a shallow 1½-quart baking dish, combine 1 can (15 oz.) **cannellini** (white kidney beans) and their liquid, the bacon mixture, 1 teaspoon **beef stock base,** 1 tablespoon tomato-based chili sauce, ¼ cup chopped **parsley,** and 1 **Polish sausage** cut in ¼-inch slices. On top, place 2 **hip-block lamb chops** (about ¾ lb. total). Cover and bake in a 375° oven for 30 minutes; remove cover and bake for 10 to 15 minutes longer or until chops brown lightly. Remove from oven and skim fat from juices. Reset oven to 400°.

Meanwhile, melt 1 tablespoon **butter** or margarine in a small frying pan. Add 1 slice **firm white bread,** crumbled, and stir until well coated; spoon over casserole. Continue to bake, uncovered, in a 400° oven for 10 minutes or until crumbs are crisp and brown.

Braised Lamb in Lemon Sauce

Trim excess fat from about 1 pound **boneless lamb** (the shank end and trimmings); cut meat into 1-inch pieces. Heat 1 tablespoon **salad oil** in a 3-quart pan over medium heat; add meat and brown well on all sides.

Stir in 1 medium-size **onion,** sliced, and 1 clove **garlic,** minced or pressed; cook until onion is limp. Add ½ teaspoon **oregano leaves,** dash of **pepper,** 1 **beef bouillon cube,** and ¾ cup **water.** Bring to boiling, reduce heat, cover, and simmer for 50 minutes or until meat is fork tender. Add 1 *each* medium-size **zucchini** and **crookneck squash,** thinly sliced. Cover; simmer for 6 to 8 minutes or until vegetables are fork tender.

With a slotted spoon, transfer meat and vegetables to a warm serving dish.

Beat 1 **egg** and ½ teaspoon **cornstarch** until blended; stir in 1 tablespoon **lemon juice.** Gradually stir hot cooking liquid into egg mixture. Return to pan and cook over low heat, stirring, until sauce thickens. Season with **salt** and **pepper** to taste, then pour over meat and vegetables. Garnish with 1 thinly sliced **green onion.**

Rolled Herbed Lamb Roast

Mix together 2 cloves **garlic,** minced or pressed; 1 tablespoon **dry vermouth;** 2 tablespoons **Dijon mustard;** and 1 teaspoon **Italian herb seasoning** (or ½ teaspoon *each* **oregano leaves** and **dry basil**). Spread over all sides of the **boneless center-cut leg of lamb** (2½ to 3 lb.). Roll up compactly; tie securely in several places. Place roast, fat side up, on a rack in a roasting pan. Insert a meat thermometer in thickest portion.

Roast, uncovered, in a 325° oven until meat thermometer registers 150° for medium rare (about 30 minutes per lb.). Remove to a serving platter.

Add ¾ cup **water** to pan drippings; scrape up browned bits from pan bottom and heat. Skim fat and pass juices at table to spoon over sliced lamb. Makes 4 to 6 servings.

Rack of Lamb for Two

⏱ *Preparation time: 5 minutes. Cooking time: 35 minutes*

Picture an intimate dinner for two—starring a rack of lamb with four small chops for each of you. The size is perfect. Accompany with asparagus spears, broccoli, and shrimp-stuffed tomatoes (page 15). A scoop of vanilla ice cream with a little creme de menthe poured over makes a quick dessert. (See cover photograph.)

1½ tablespoons butter or margarine, at room temperature
1 tablespoon minced parsley
1 small clove garlic, minced or pressed
    Dash of salt and pepper
8-rib rack of lamb, Frenched (meat removed from ends of long chop bones)

Mix together butter, parsley, garlic, and salt and pepper until well blended. Rub mixture over lamb and place in a shallow roasting pan with rib bones pointing downward. Insert meat thermometer in thickest part of roast without touching bone.

Roast in a 425° oven for 35 minutes or until meat thermometer reaches 145° for medium-rare.

To serve, cut lamb between ribs. Four chops make 1 serving.

Miniature Moussaka

⏱ *Preparation time: 35 minutes. Cooking time: 20 minutes*

A golden cheese layer tops a traditional eggplant moussaka. Assemble this ground lamb and eggplant casserole in a shallow baking dish or a medium-size (about 4½ by 8-inch) loaf pan.

1 small (¾ to 1 lb.) eggplant
    About 3 tablespoons olive oil or salad oil
½ pound lean ground lamb or ground beef
½ cup chopped onion
1 clove garlic, minced or pressed
1 can (8 oz.) stewed tomatoes
1 can (2 oz.) mushroom stems and pieces
¼ cup catsup
¼ teaspoon *each* oregano leaves and ground cinnamon
2 tablespoons minced parsley
1 cup (about 4 oz.) shredded jack cheese
2 tablespoons grated Parmesan cheese

Rinse eggplant and pat dry; cut off and discard stem end and cut eggplant into ½-inch-thick slices. Brush eggplant slices liberally on both sides with oil; arrange in a single layer in a shallow pan. Bake in a 475° oven, turning if needed, until eggplant slices are well browned on both sides (about 30 minutes).

Meanwhile, in a wide frying pan over medium-high heat, cook ground meat until browned and crumbly. Add onion and garlic and cook for about 5 minutes until onion is limp. Discard any excess fat. Add tomatoes (break them up with a spoon), mushrooms and their liquid, catsup, oregano, cinnamon, and parsley. Cook, uncovered, over medium heat until sauce is thick (about 10 minutes).

Arrange ½ the eggplant in bottom of a shallow 1-quart baking dish, spoon over ½ the meat sauce, and sprinkle with ½ of the jack cheese. Repeat layers, using remaining eggplant, meat sauce, and jack cheese.

Sprinkle Parmesan cheese evenly over top. Bake, uncovered, in a 375° oven for about 20 minutes or until browned and bubbly.

Make-ahead Lamb Stew

⏱ *Preparation time: 25 minutes. Cooking time: 1 hour and 35 minutes*

To make this classic lamb stew ahead, cook it as directed, then refrigerate. Just before dinner time, reheat it slowly to serve with a crisp green salad and crusty French rolls. For dessert, serve wedges of honeydew melon with a squeeze of fresh lime.

1 pound lean boneless lamb stew meat, cut in 1-inch cubes
1½ tablespoons olive oil or salad oil
1 small clove garlic, minced or pressed
¾ cup regular-strength chicken broth
½ cup dry white wine (or additional chicken broth)
¼ teaspoon *each* rubbed sage and grated lemon peel
¼ teaspoon *each* marjoram and savory leaves
2 medium-size carrots
¼ pound small white boiling onions
3 small new potatoes (about 6 oz.), cut in ½-inch-thick slices
    Chopped parsley

Trim excess fat and membrane from lamb. Heat oil in a wide frying pan over medium-high heat; add lamb and cook, uncovered, until well browned on all sides. Add garlic and cook, stirring, until lightly browned. Stir in chicken broth, wine, sage, lemon peel, marjoram, and savory. Cover and simmer for 1 hour.

Meanwhile, cut carrots diagonally in 1-inch lengths. Plunge onions into boiling water for about 1

minute; drain and peel. When lamb has simmered for 1 hour, add carrots, onions, and potato slices to the pan, then cover and simmer until vegetables are fork tender (about 35 minutes more).

With a slotted spoon, lift vegetables and meat from pan and place in individual bowls or deep plates. Turn heat to high and boil, uncovered, to reduce liquid to about ½ cup. Pour over stew. Sprinkle with parsley.

Sweet and Sour Stew

⏱ *Preparation time: 20 minutes. Cooking time: 1 hour and 55 minutes*

A rich red sauce develops from the catsup-based sweet and sour mixture used as a cooking broth for lean beef or lamb stew meat. Serve with crusty French bread to soak up the juices. (See photograph on facing page.)

> 2 tablespoons all-purpose flour
> 1 teaspoon salt
> Dash of pepper
> 1 pound boneless, lean lamb stew meat or beef chuck, cut in 1-inch cubes
> 1½ tablespoons butter or margarine
> ¼ cup catsup
> 2 tablespoons *each* packed brown sugar and red wine vinegar
> 1½ teaspoons Worcestershire
> ½ cup water
> 6 small white boiling onions, peeled
> 2 large carrots, cut in 1-inch chunks
> Chopped parsley

Combine flour, ½ teaspoon of the salt, and pepper. Dredge meat pieces in flour mixture, shaking off excess.

In a deep 3 to 4-quart pan, melt butter over medium-high heat; add meat and brown well on all sides. Drain off and discard excess fat. Combine catsup, brown sugar, vinegar, Worcestershire, water, and remaining ½ teaspoon salt; add to meat. Add onions and simmer, covered, for 1 hour and 15 minutes, stirring once or twice. Add carrots and cook for about 40 minutes longer or until meat and vegetables are fork tender. Sprinkle with parsley.

SWEET AND SOUR STEW, richly laden with small onions and carrots, cooks unattended for several hours (recipe above). Serve this hearty dish with hunks of sourdough bread, garlic herb-flavored cheese, and radishes.

Oven-barbecued Country-style Spareribs

⏱ *Preparation time: 15 minutes. Cooking time: 2 hours*

Plan on 2 hours for cooking thick, meaty spareribs topped first with lemon and onion, then with a well-seasoned sauce. Accompany the tangy ribs with crusty rolls and a butter lettuce salad.

> 1 to 1½ pounds country-style spareribs, trimmed of surface fat
> ½ lemon, thinly sliced
> 1 small onion, thinly sliced
> 2 tablespoons packed brown sugar
> 1 teaspoon chili powder
> ¼ teaspoon *each* celery seed and garlic salt
> ½ cup water
> ⅓ cup tomato-based chili sauce
> 2 tablespoons vinegar
> 1½ teaspoons *each* Worcestershire and soy sauce

Arrange spareribs in a single layer in an 8-inch-square baking dish. Distribute lemon and onion evenly over meat. Cover and bake in a 350° oven for 1 hour and 15 minutes.

Meanwhile, in a pan combine brown sugar, chili powder, celery seed, garlic salt, water, chili sauce, vinegar, Worcestershire, and soy sauce. Cook, uncovered, over medium heat for 5 minutes.

Remove lemon and onion slices and discard. Lift ribs from pan and cut in serving-size pieces. Discard pan drippings. Return meat to pan and pour hot sauce over. Continue baking, uncovered, basting frequently, for about 45 minutes or until meat is glazed and fork tender. Transfer meat to a serving dish. Skim off and discard any fat from sauce. Spoon sauce over meat.

Polish Sausage and Potatoes

⏱ *Preparation time (cooking included): 30 minutes*

You use the same frying pan to cook each of the elements for this hearty entrée—start by browning the sausage, and while it cooks, prepare the vegetables and apple. Serve the sausage with mustard and horseradish, and a sliced tomato and cucumber salad with oil and vinegar dressing.

> About 6 tablespoons butter or margarine
> 8 to 10 ounces kielbasa
> 2 medium-size potatoes, peeled and thinly sliced
> 1 large onion, thinly sliced
> 1 large Golden Delicious apple

(Continued on next page)

Melt 1 tablespoon of the butter in a wide frying pan over medium heat. Slash sausage at 1-inch intervals and cook until browned on all sides. Arrange on a warm serving dish; keep warm.

Add 4 tablespoons of the butter to pan; add potatoes and onion and stir well. Cover and cook, turning often and adding more butter, if needed, until potatoes are tender (about 15 minutes).

Remove lid and continue cooking until potatoes are browned; arrange with sausage; keep warm.

Peel and core apple; cut into ½-inch-thick rings. Melt 1 more tablespoon butter in pan; add apple rings and cook until lightly browned on both sides. Arrange with sausage and potatoes.

Sweet and Sour Pork

⏱ *Preparation time (cooking included): 30 minutes*

A favorite among lovers of Chinese food, sweet and sour pork has endless variations. The one that follows is both quick and colorful. Have all the vegetables cut up and the sweet and sour sauce ready to go before you begin cooking.

- ¾ **pound lean boneless pork, cut in 1-inch cubes**
- 1 **egg, beaten**
  About ¼ cup cornstarch
  About 2½ tablespoons salad oil
- 1 **small onion, cut in 1-inch squares**
- 1 **medium-size carrot, sliced diagonally ¼ inch thick**
- 1 **small clove garlic, minced or pressed**
- 1 **small green pepper, seeded and cut in 1-inch squares**
- 1 **can (8¼ oz.) sliced pineapple, drained and cut in pieces, or ¾ cup fresh pineapple chunks**
- 1 **medium-size tomato, cut in 1-inch cubes**
  Sweet and sour sauce (recipe follows)

Dip pork pieces in egg, drain briefly, and roll in cornstarch until lightly coated on all sides; shake off excess. Heat 1½ tablespoons of the oil in a wide frying pan over medium-high heat. Add pork and cook, turning constantly with a wide spatula, until browned (about 7 minutes). Lift pork from pan and set aside; scrape free and discard any browned particles, leaving oil in pan.

Add enough oil to pan to make about 1 tablespoon total. Place over highest heat. Add onion, carrot, and garlic; cook, stirring, for about 3 minutes or until vegetables are tender-crisp. Add green pepper, pineapple, tomato, and sweet and sour sauce; cook, stirring, over high heat until mixture boils. Add pork, then cook and stir for 1 minute longer to heat through and coat pork with sauce.

Sweet and sour sauce. Stir together 1½ teaspoons **cornstarch** and 2½ tablespoons packed **brown sugar.** Stir in ¼ teaspoon grated **fresh ginger root** or ⅛ teaspoon ground ginger, 1½ teaspoons *each* **soy sauce** and **dry sherry,** and 2 tablespoons *each* **wine vinegar** and **water.**

Pork Tenderloin with Onion-Apple Cream

⏱ *Preparation time: 20 minutes. Cooking time: 25 minutes*

Baste a small whole pork tenderloin with sherry-flavored cream as it roasts. The same basting sauce flavors slow-cooked apples and onions. Serve green beans and warm, soft rolls alongside.

- 1 **whole pork tenderloin (about 12 oz.)**
  Sherry baste (recipe follows)
- 1 **large onion, thinly sliced**
- 1 **small Golden Delicious apple, thinly sliced**
- 2 **tablespoons butter or margarine**
  Parsley sprigs

Place pork tenderloin on rack in a broiler pan; insert meat thermometer into thickest part. Brush pork with sherry baste. Cook in a 425° oven for 25 to 30 minutes or until meat thermometer registers 170°; baste frequently during roasting.

Meanwhile, melt butter in a wide frying pan over medium heat. Add onion and apple and cook, stirring frequently, until limp and golden (about 20 minutes). Add remaining sherry baste and bring to a boil; place in a small serving bowl. Garnish meat with parsley sprigs and pass onion-apple cream to spoon over.

Sherry baste. Mix together 6 tablespoons **whipping cream,** 2 tablespoons **cream sherry,** 1 teaspoon **Dijon mustard,** and ½ teaspoon *each* **salt** and prepared **horseradish.**

Mushroom-topped Pork Chops

🕐 *Preparation time: 10 minutes. Cooking time: 30 minutes*

Add fresh mushrooms to mushroom soup and you have a supereasy, mellow sauce for pan-fried pork chops.

4 **center cut loin pork chops, cut 1 inch thick**
Pepper
½ **pound mushrooms, sliced**
1 **can (10½ oz.) condensed cream of mushroom soup**

Trim fat from chops; add a piece of fat to a wide frying pan. Cook over medium heat until pan is well greased; discard fat. Add pork chops, sprinkle with pepper, and cook over medium heat until browned on both sides; remove from pan. Add mushrooms to pan and cook, stirring, until lightly browned and liquid has evaporated; stir in soup. Arrange chops in sauce. Cook, covered, over low heat for about 30 minutes or until meat is fork tender.

Pork Chops with Rhubarb Dressing

🕐 *Preparation time: 15 minutes. Cooking time: 1 hour*

Rhubarb cooks down to make a sweet-sour sauce for both chops and dressing. Complete the meal with fresh buttered peas, and ice cream for dessert.

⅛ **teaspoon dry rosemary, crumbled**
½ **teaspoon salt**
Dash pepper
2 **pork loin or shoulder chops, cut ¾ inch thick**
1 **tablespoon salad oil**
2 **slices firm-textured bread, cut into ½-inch cubes (about 1¾ cups)**
⅓ **cup firmly packed brown sugar**
¼ **teaspoon ground cinnamon**
⅛ **teaspoon ground allspice**
1 **pound rhubarb, cut into ½-inch pieces (about 3 cups)**
1½ **tablespoons all-purpose flour**

Mix together rosemary, salt, and pepper. Sprinkle evenly over chops. Heat oil in a wide frying pan over medium-high heat; add chops and brown on both sides; set aside with drippings.

Stir together bread cubes, brown sugar, cinnamon, allspice, rhubarb, and flour; spread half the mixture in a greased shallow 1½ to 2-quart baking dish. Arrange chops on top; spoon over 2 tablespoons drippings (add water if necessary, to make this amount); top with remaining rhubarb mixture. Cover and refrigerate if made ahead. Bake, covered, in a 350° oven for 45 minutes; then uncover and bake for 15 minutes longer or until pork is fork tender.

Linguisa and Garbanzo Stew

🕐 *Preparation time: 15 minutes. Cooking time: 30 minutes*

Unlike some stews, this one needs only a half-hour of simmering to be ready for the table. Canned garbanzos contribute to the speed, and sausage lends its piquant flavor.

1 **tablespoon olive oil or salad oil**
1 **small onion, chopped**
2 **cups shredded cabbage**
1 **can (about 1 lb.) garbanzos**
About ½ pound linguisa or Polish sausage
1 **hard-cooked egg, thinly sliced or pressed through a sieve**
Pitted ripe olives

Heat oil in a wide frying pan over medium heat; add onion and cabbage and cook, stirring, until vegetables are limp and lightly browned. Stir in garbanzos and their liquid. Cut linguisa into 2-inch chunks and add to pan. Cover and simmer for 30 minutes, stirring occasionally. Skim and discard fat. Ladle into soup plates and garnish with hard-cooked egg and olives.

From the simplest oven-fried chicken thighs to the grandest Cornish hens—plump and somehow complete in miniature, under a flaming cherry sauce—poultry appears to have been designed expressly to accommodate the for-two cook. As if the availability of small birds weren't enough of a boon, it's a simple matter in most markets to buy only the pieces you need and like best; and nowadays that's true not just of chicken but even of turkey, once the province of only the most patient eaters of leftovers.

In this chapter you'll find recipes for cooking chicken with fruits, vegetables, nuts, surprising seasonings, fragrant sauces. Cornish hens appear in two versions, turkey meat in three.

The amounts of poultry you'll buy will depend on your appetite and on what other ingredients are going into the meal. Quantities specified in our recipes reflect the latter variable, and with a little experimenting you'll solve the former.

General rules are that a 2 to 2½-pound broiler-fryer is ample for two; a large whole chicken breast serves two, though you may prefer to offer one small breast apiece. Two small Cornish hens serve two generously; a single large one would also serve two. A duck—with high fat content that makes it unique among birds—will lose much fat as it cooks, so that a 4 to 5-pound duckling will yield only 2 to 3 servings.

Crusty Oven-fried Chicken

⏱ *Preparation time: 15 minutes. Cooking time: 1 hour*

Soy-marinated chicken is coated with seasoned crumbs and sesame seed, then baked to crispy doneness in the oven (See photograph on facing page.)

- ¼ cup soy sauce
- 1 tablespoon salad oil
- 1 small clove garlic, minced or pressed
- 2 to 4 chicken legs with thighs attached (about ½ lb. *each*)
- ¼ cup wheat germ
- 2 tablespoons fine dry bread crumbs
- 1 tablespoon *each* sesame seed and chopped parsley
- ¼ teaspoon *each* pepper and paprika
  Parsley (optional)

Combine soy sauce, oil, and garlic. Arrange chicken in a single layer in a shallow baking dish. Pour soy mixture over chicken, turn chicken to coat all sides, and let stand for about 10 minutes.

Meanwhile, mix together wheat germ, bread crumbs, sesame seed, chopped parsley, pepper, and paprika.

Lift chicken from marinade, drain, then turn over in wheat germ mixture to evenly coat all sides; shake off excess. Arrange coated chicken on a well-greased rimmed baking sheet. Bake, uncovered, in a 350° oven for about 1 hour or until thigh meat near bone is no longer pink when slashed. Remove to serving platter and garnish with parsley, if desired.

Curried Chicken

⏱ *Preparation time: 10 minutes. Cooking time: 35 minutes*

Each of you gets a chicken half, butter-broiled to succulency. Broiling eliminates messy pan-frying and the cleanup that follows.

- 2 tablespoons butter or margarine, at room temperature
- 1 tablespoon curry powder
- ¼ teaspoon *each* ground ginger and ground cloves
  Dash *each* salt and pepper
- 2 to 2½ pound broiler-fryer chicken, split in half
- ½ cup dry white wine, dry vermouth, or regular-strength chicken broth

(Continued on next page)

FINGER-FOOD DINNER features sesame seed coated oven-fried chicken (recipe above), French fried potatoes, and whole fresh fruit.

In a small bowl, combine butter, curry powder, ginger, cloves, salt, and pepper. With a sharp knife, cut several small slits in skin of chicken over breasts and thighs. Push about ¾ of the butter mixture in between skin and flesh.

Melt remaining butter mixture and stir in white wine. Place chicken halves, skin side down, on rack in broiler pan. Broil 6 to 8 inches below heat for 20 minutes, basting several times with wine mixture. Turn chicken pieces over and continue broiling and basting for 15 to 20 minutes or until meat is no longer pink when slashed in thickest part.

Transfer chicken to serving platter. Skim and discard fat from pan juices, then pour juices over chicken.

Chicken Sauté with Green Beans

⏱ *Preparation time: 10 minutes. Cooking time: 50 minutes*

Chicken sautéed with green beans makes its own sauce, simmering in cream and wine. Serve it with parsley-buttered potatoes and vegetable relishes.

- ½ **teaspooon salt**
  Dash pepper
- 2 **tablespoons all-purpose flour**
- 2 **to 2½-pound broiler-fryer, cut in quarters**
- 1½ **tablespoons butter or margarine**
- ¼ **pound mushrooms, sliced**
- 1 **tablespoon freeze-dried shallots**
- ⅓ **cup** *each* **whipping cream and dry white wine**
- 1 **cup frozen cut green beans, thawed**
  Walnut halves (optional)

Mix together salt, pepper, and flour. Dredge chicken in mixture to coat; shake off excess. In a wide frying pan over medium heat, melt butter; add chicken and brown well on all sides, adding more butter, if needed (about 15 minutes). Stir in mushrooms, shallots, cream, and wine. Cover and simmer for 25 minutes. Add beans, cover, and simmer for 10 to 15 minutes or just until meat is no longer pink when slashed in thickest part. Remove chicken and vegetables to a serving dish. Boil cooking liquid, uncovered, until slightly thickened. Pour sauce over chicken and vegetables. Garnish with walnuts, if you wish.

Chicken sauté for one. Use 1 quarter of a 3 to 3½-pound **chicken.** Sprinkle with **salt** and **pepper** to taste and enough all-purpose **flour** to coat lightly. Cook in 1 tablespoon **butter,** adding 3 sliced **mushrooms,** 2 teaspoons chopped **shallots,** ¼ cup *each* **whipping cream** and dry **white wine,** and ½ cup frozen cut **green beans.**

Simple Pâté

When you want a little appetizer before dinner, think of this chicken liver pâté. Save the livers from just two chickens (they freeze well). Serve pâté on Melba toast.

In a frying pan over medium-low heat, cook 2 **chicken livers** in 1 tablespoon **butter** or margarine until just pink in center when slashed (about 5 minutes). In a blender or food processor, chop livers with butter and ⅓ of a small package (3-oz. size) **cream cheese,** a few drops **liquid hot pepper seasoning,** ¼ teaspoon **salt,** 1 tablespoon chopped **green pepper,** and 1 teaspoon **dry sherry.** Cover and chill. Serve with **Melba toast** or crisp rye crackers. Makes ⅓ cup.

Chicken with Artichokes

⏱ *Preparation time: 15 minutes. Cooking time : 20-40 minutes*

An attractive chicken dish is this one baked with artichoke hearts and sliced mushrooms and flavored with sherry. Serve with rice, if you wish.

- 2 **whole chicken breasts (about ¾ lb.** *each***), split, or 2** *each* **legs and thighs**
  Salt, pepper, and paprika
  About 1 tablespoon *each* **butter or margarine and salad oil**
- 1 **package (about 9 oz.) frozen artichoke hearts, thawed**
- 5 **medium-size mushrooms, sliced**
- 4 **teaspoons all-purpose flour**
- ½ **cup water**
- 2 **tablespoons dry sherry**
- 1 **teaspoon chicken stock base**
- ⅛ **teaspoon dry rosemary, crumbled**
  Minced parsley

Sprinkle chicken lightly with salt, pepper, and paprika. In a wide frying pan, cook chicken in butter and oil over medium-high heat until browned. Arrange chicken in a 1 to 1½-quart casserole with artichoke hearts.

Cook mushrooms in pan drippings until liquid evaporates; sprinkle mushrooms with flour and stir to blend. Gradually stir in water, sherry, chicken stock base, and rosemary. Cook, stirring, until slightly thickened; pour over chicken. Cover and bake in a 375° oven for 20 minutes for breasts (40 minutes for legs) or until meat is no longer pink when slashed in thickest part. Garnish with minced parsley.

Chicken with Sweet Onions

🕐 *Preparation time: 20 minutes. Cooking time: 25 to 45 minutes*

Generously topped with flavorful onions and toasted almonds, your choice of meaty chicken pieces—dark or light—will make a beautiful, easy baked dish.

    3 tablespoons slivered almonds
    ½ teaspoon salt
      Dash *each* pepper and paprika
      About 1½ pounds meaty chicken pieces
    2 tablespoons butter or margarine
    2 large onions, thinly sliced
    1 tablespoon packed brown sugar
    ¼ teaspoon ground cinnamon
      Lemon wedges

Spread almonds in a shallow pan and toast in a 350° oven for 8 to 10 minutes or until golden; set aside.

Mix together salt, pepper, and paprika; sprinkle evenly over chicken. Arrange chicken, skin side down, in a shallow greased 2-quart baking dish. Bake, uncovered, in a 400° oven 30 minutes for dark meat, 15 minutes for white meat. Turn meat over and bake 15 minutes for dark meat, 10 minutes for white meat or until no longer pink when slashed in thickest part.

Meanwhile, melt butter in wide frying pan over medium-low heat. Add onion, separating into rings, and cook slowly, uncovered, stirring often, until onion is limp and golden (about 30 minutes); onion should not show signs of browning during first 15 minutes—if it does, reduce heat. Sprinkle with brown sugar and cinnamon; stir to blend.

Cover chicken with onion mixture, sprinkle with toasted almonds, and serve with lemon wedges to squeeze over servings.

Chicken Cacciatore

🕐 *Preparation time: 15 minutes. Cooking time: 50 minutes*

This familiar Italian dish cooks in less than an hour, yet achieves a traditionally robust flavor. The chicken and sauce are good with green noodles.

    1 tablespoon butter or margarine
    1 tablespoon olive oil
    2 whole chicken legs with thighs attached (about
      ½ lb. *each*)
    ¼ pound mushrooms, sliced
    1 small onion, sliced
    1 green pepper, seeded and finely chopped
    1 clove garlic, minced or pressed
    ¼ cup dry white wine or regular-strength chicken
      broth
    1 can (8 oz.) tomato sauce
    ¾ teaspoon salt
    ⅛ teaspoon *each* marjoram, oregano, and thyme
      leaves, crumbled
    ½ teaspoon chicken stock base
    1 tablespoon minced parsley

Heat butter and oil in a wide frying pan over medium-high heat. Add chicken and cook, turning, until browned on all sides; remove from pan and set aside. Add mushrooms, onion, green pepper, and garlic to pan drippings and cook, stirring, until onion is limp (about 5 minutes). Stir in wine, tomato sauce, salt, marjoram, oregano, thyme, stock base, and parsley.

Return chicken to pan. Bring liquid to boiling, reduce heat, cover, and simmer for about 40 minutes or until meat is no longer pink when slashed in thickest part. If sauce is too thin, remove chicken to a serving dish and keep warm; bring sauce to a boil, then cook, uncovered, stirring, until slightly thickened. Pour over chicken.

Chicken with New Potatoes and Carrots

🕐 *Preparation time: 10 minutes. Cooking time: 50 minutes*

Everything for dinner bakes together in the oven. You can even bake dessert—frozen fruit turnovers to serve flaky and hot with ice cream—at the same time.

    2 tablespoons *each* fine dry bread crumbs and
      yellow cornmeal
    ¾ teaspoon curry powder
    ⅛ teaspoon salt
      Dash pepper
    2 to 2½-pound broiler-fryer chicken, cut in
      quarters
    ¼ cup butter or margarine
    4 small carrots, peeled
    4 small whole new potatoes (*each* about 1½
      inches in diameter)
      Chopped parsley

(Continued on next page)

In a small bag combine crumbs, cornmeal, curry powder, salt, and pepper. Shake chicken quarters, 1 at a time, in bag to coat completely; set aside. In a 9 by 13-inch baking dish, melt butter in oven while it is preheating to 400°. Tilt pan slightly so butter collects in one corner; roll carrots and potatoes in butter to coat evenly, then push to one side. Coat chicken with butter, laying pieces skin side down beside vegetables.

Bake, uncovered, in a 400° oven for 30 minutes. Turn vegetables and chicken over and bake for 20 minutes longer or until vegetables are fork tender and chicken is no longer pink when slashed in thickest part. Sprinkle with parsley.

Chicken Breasts Veronique

🕐 *Preparation time: 15 minutes. Cooking time: 25 minutes*

For a special occasion, serve this elegant dish that's highlighted by a delicate cream sauce and seedless green grapes; sautéed whole mushrooms are the garnish. Just add a butter lettuce salad. (See photograph on facing page.)

> 2 **whole chicken breasts (about ¾ lb. *each*), split, boned, and skinned**
> **Salt**
> 3 **tablespoons butter or margarine**
> 1 **tablespoon orange marmalade**
> ¼ **teaspoon tarragon, crumbled**
> ¼ **cup dry white wine**
> 8 **medium-size mushrooms, fluted, and stems trimmed**
> ¼ **cup whipping cream**
> ½ **teaspoon cornstarch**
> 2 **teaspoons water**
> ¾ **cup seedless grapes**
> **Parsley sprigs**

Sprinkle chicken lightly with salt. Melt 1 tablespoon of the butter in wide frying pan over medium heat. Add chicken breasts and cook until golden on each side. Stir in marmalade, tarragon, and wine. Cover and simmer for about 15 minutes or until meat is no longer pink when slashed in thickest part. Transfer to warm serving dish.

Meanwhile, melt remaining 2 tablespoons butter in a small pan, over medium heat. Add mushrooms and cook, stirring, until liquid evaporates.

To pan juices add cream and quickly bring to a full rolling boil. Blend cornstarch with water; stir into sauce. Return sauce to a boil, stirring. Mix in grapes, return to a boil, then pour sauce over chicken. Garnish with sautéed mushrooms and parsley sprigs.

Chicken breast veronique for one. Use 1 whole **chicken breast,** 2 teaspoons *each* **butter** or margarine and **marmalade,** ⅛ teaspoon **tarragon,** 2 tablespoons *each* dry **white wine** and **whipping cream,** ¼ teaspoon **cornstarch,** 1 teaspoon **water,** and ⅓ cup **seedless grapes.** Cook 4 whole **mushrooms** in 1 tablespoon **butter** or margarine.

Chicken Scallopini

🕐 *Preparation time: 10 minutes. Cooking time: 7 minutes*

Boned chicken breasts are a versatile ingredient, ideal for a quick but special dinner for two. Try them pounded and cooked as scallopini with either a brandy cream sauce or a lemon mustard sauce. Both are delicious with broccoli or asparagus spears.

> 2 **whole chicken breasts (about ¾ lb. *each*), split, boned, and skinned**
> 2 to 3 **tablespoons butter or margarine**
> **Salt and pepper**
> 2 **tablespoons brandy**
> ¼ **cup whipping cream**

Place chicken breasts, cut side down, about 5 to 6 inches apart between 2 sheets of clear plastic wrap or wax paper. Pound with smooth side of a mallet until pieces are no more than ⅛ inch thick.

In a wide frying pan, melt 2 tablespoons of the butter over medium-high heat. Add chicken breasts and cook, uncovered, until lightly browned on each side, adding more butter if needed to prevent sticking. Sprinkle chicken with salt and pepper.

Warm brandy in a small container, pour over chicken, and at once set aflame (*not under an exhaust fan or flammable items*); shake pan until flame dies.

Remove from heat and with a slotted spoon quickly lift chicken from juices to a serving dish; keep warm. Return frying pan to highest heat and add cream. Boil rapidly, uncovered, scraping up browned particles, until large shiny bubbles form. Drain any accumulated juices from chicken into sauce, then spoon over chicken and serve.

Chicken with lemon mustard sauce. Follow recipe for chicken scallopini (preceding), making these changes: Instead of brandy, use 2 tablespoons **lemon juice;** omit flaming. Add 2 teaspoons **Dijon mustard** with **whipping cream.**

(Continued on page 52)

DELICATE TARRAGON CREAM SAUCE, accented with green grapes and fluted mushrooms, flows over boned chicken breasts (recipe at left). Serve with butter lettuce salad and vinaigrette dressing (page 15).

Chicken with lemon mustard sauce for one. Use 1 whole chicken breast, split; brown it in about 1 tablespoon **butter** or margarine. Use 1 tablespoon **lemon juice,** 2 to 3 tablespoons **whipping cream,** and 1 teaspoon **Dijon mustard.**

Slivered Chicken and Walnuts

⏱ *Preparation time (cooking included): 10 minutes*

Dinner is on the table in minutes when you stir-fry. Assemble chicken, nuts, ginger, and seasoning sauce; then cook and eat.

> Cooking sauce (recipe follows)
> 1 **whole chicken breast (about 1 lb.), boned and skinned**
> 1 **tablespoon soy sauce**
> 1 **teaspoon cornstarch**
> 3 **tablespoons salad oil**
> ½ **cup walnut halves**
> 1 **medium-size green pepper, seeded and cut into 1-inch squares**
> ½ **teaspoon finely minced fresh ginger or ¼ teaspoon ground ginger**

Prepare cooking sauce; set aside. Cut chicken into thin strips; mix with soy and cornstarch and set aside.

Heat oil over medium-high heat in a wok or wide frying pan; add nuts and cook, stirring, until brown; remove with slotted spoon. Add chicken to oil; cook, stirring, until opaque (about 1½ minutes); lift out. Add pepper and ginger; cook, stirring, until pepper is bright green. Add chicken and cooking sauce; cook, stirring, until thick (about 1 minute); add nuts and serve.

Cooking sauce. Thoroughly blend ½ teaspoon **cornstarch,** dash **liquid hot pepper seasoning,** ¾ teaspoon *each* **sugar** and **wine vinegar,** 1 teaspoon **dry sherry** or water, and 1 tablespoon **soy sauce.**

Spicy Barbecued Chicken

⏱ *Preparation time: 10 minutes. Marinating time: 4 hours. Heat coals: 35 minutes. Cooking time: 40 minutes*

In the morning or the night before, start the chicken legs marinating in a spicy Pakistani-style yogurt mixture for barbecuing in the evening. Serve them with cool tomato-cucumber sauce—this, too, can be made ahead. Add a butter lettuce salad and fresh fruit.

> 2 **whole chicken legs with thighs attached (about ½ lb. *each*)**
> ⅓ **cup unflavored yogurt**
> ¼ **teaspoon ground ginger**
> ½ **teaspoon *each* salt and garlic powder**
> ⅛ **teaspoon cayenne**
> 1 **tablespoon lemon juice**
> **Lemon wedges**
> **Tomato-cucumber sauce (recipe follows)**

Remove chicken skin, if you wish. Slash each piece of chicken 2 or 3 times about halfway to the bone; place in a shallow, close-fitting pan. Combine yogurt, ginger, salt, garlic powder, cayenne, and lemon juice; pour over chicken, cover, and refrigerate for 4 to 6 hours or until next day, turning occasionally, if possible.

Lift chicken from marinade, drain briefly, and place on a barbecue grill about 6 inches above a solid bed of low-glowing coals. Cook, turning and lightly brushing with marinade, until meat is well browned on all sides and no longer pink when slashed in thickest part (40 to 50 minutes). Serve with lemon wedges and tomato-cucumber sauce to spoon over.

Tomato-cucumber sauce. Stir together ½ cup **unflavored yogurt;** 1 small **tomato,** peeled and finely diced; ½ cup finely diced, peeled **cucumber;** 2 thinly sliced **green onions** (including some green tops); ½ teaspoon ground **cumin;** ¼ teaspoon **salt;** and 1 tablespoon finely chopped fresh **coriander** (cilantro—or use 1 teaspoon dried cilantro), watercress, or mint. Cover and chill thoroughly. Makes about ¾ cup.

cream until smooth. Pour into pan; cook and stir over medium heat until sauce thickens. Pour sauce over chicken and sprinkle with green onion.

Garlic Chicken and New Potatoes

🕐 *Preparation time: 10 minutes. Cooking time: 45 minutes*

Slow cooking transforms the raw harshness of garlic into a sweetness so mild that you can use it in generous quantities. The chicken cooks on top of the range along with new potatoes—all steeping in garlic.

    2 tablespoons olive oil or salad oil
    2 chicken legs with thighs attached (about ½ lb.
       each)
    4 small new potatoes (about 2 inches in diameter)
       or 2 medium-size potatoes (about 4 inches in
       diameter), cut in half
    ½ teaspoon dry rosemary
    2 tablespoons water
   12 cloves garlic, slightly crushed
       Salt and pepper

Heat oil in a wide frying pan over medium-high heat and add chicken and potatoes. Cook, turning potatoes occasionally and chicken once, until chicken is browned on both sides (about 15 minutes).

Reduce heat to low and add rosemary and water; cover and cook for 15 minutes. Turn chicken and potatoes over and add garlic. Cover and cook, turning potatoes and garlic occasionally, until meat is no longer pink when slashed in thickest part (about 15 minutes). Transfer chicken and potatoes to serving dish. Add salt and pepper to taste.

Chicken Liver Mushroom Sauté

🕐 *Preparation time: 5 minutes. Cooking time: 7 minutes*

For a brunch or quick supper, serve chicken liver sauté over toasted English muffins.

    2 to 3 tablespoons butter or margarine
      ¾ pound chicken livers, halved
      ¼ pound mushrooms, quartered
    1½ teaspoons all-purpose flour
      ¼ teaspoon each fines herbes and salt
      2 tablespoons dry sherry
      ¼ cup regular-strength chicken broth
      2 English muffins, split and buttered
         Chopped parsley

(Continued on page 55)

Tarragon Chicken

🕐 *Preparation time: 10 minutes. Cooking time: 30 minutes*

Nice to serve with fluffy rice is this creamy entrée using chicken breasts. Add buttered carrots, cooked tender-crisp, for a colorful complement.

    2 tablespoons all-purpose flour
    ½ teaspoon salt
       Dash pepper
    2 whole chicken breasts (about ¾ lb. each), split
   1½ tablespoons butter or margarine
    1 small onion, chopped
    ¼ pound mushrooms, sliced
    ½ cup dry white wine or regular-strength chicken
       broth
    ¼ teaspoon each sugar and tarragon, crumbled
    ½ cup sour cream
    1 green onion, thinly sliced (including some of
       green top)

Mix flour with salt and pepper; dredge chicken in mixture to coat; shake off excess and set aside extra flour. Heat butter in a wide frying pan over medium-high heat. Add chicken and cook, uncovered, turning to brown lightly on all sides; remove from pan and set aside. Add onion and mushrooms to pan drippings and cook until onion is limp (about 5 minutes). Stir in wine, sugar, and tarragon. Return chicken to pan. Cover and simmer for about 20 minutes or until meat is no longer pink when slashed in thickest part. Remove chicken from pan and keep warm.

Mix 1 teaspoon of the reserved flour with sour

Melt 2 tablespoons of the butter in a wide frying pan over medium-high heat. Add livers and mushrooms and cook just until livers are browned, adding more butter if needed. Stir in flour, fines herbes, and salt; remove from heat and gradually stir in sherry and chicken broth. Return to heat and cook, stirring, for about 3 minutes or until thickened.

Meanwhile, toast muffins in a toaster oven or broiler. Serve chicken livers over muffins; sprinkle with parsley.

Game Hens with Flaming Cherry Sauce

⏱ *Thaw frozen birds. Preparation time: 10 minutes. Cooking time: 1 hour*

Flaming a dish at the table is dramatic enough for the most special occasion, easy enough for everyday. And Cornish hens make any dinner seem festive. (See photograph on facing page.)

   2 **Rock Cornish game hens (16 to 20 oz. e*ach*)**
      Seasoned salt and pepper
   2 **tablespoons butter or margarine, melted**
   ½ **teaspoon e*ach* seasoned salt, ground ginger, and paprika**
      Cherry sauce (recipe follows)
      Orange slices
   2 **tablespoons brandy (optional)**

Thaw hens as directed on package (set giblets aside for other uses); rinse hens and pat dry. Sprinkle inside cavities with seasoned salt and pepper. Place hens slightly apart, breast sides up, in a roasting pan.

Combine butter with the ½ teaspoon seasoned salt, ginger, and paprika; brush over hens, using it all. Bake hens, uncovered, in a 350° oven for about 1 hour or until leg joints move easily; during last half hour, baste birds several times with pan drippings. Meanwhile, prepare cherry sauce; keep warm over low heat or in a chafing dish.

When hens are roasted, discard excess fat from pan juices and stir juices into cherry sauce. Arrange hens on serving plates and garnish with orange slices; keep warm. To flame birds, warm brandy in a small container; ignite (not under an exhaust fan or flammable items) and pour, flaming, into sauce. While still flaming, spoon sauce over birds.

FOR A DRAMATIC ENTRÉE, flame Cornish game hens with brandied cherry sauce at the table just before serving (recipe above). Allow one hen per hungry diner and let orange slices and broccoli spears round out the menu.

Cherry sauce. Drain 1 small can (about 8 oz.) pitted **dark sweet cherries,** reserving ⅓ cup syrup. In a pan, combine reserved syrup with ⅔ cup **water, 1 chicken bouillon cube, 1** small **onion** (cut in wedges), 8 whole **cloves,** and ¼ teaspoon ground **cinnamon.** Bring to a boil, stirring; then reduce heat and simmer, uncovered, for 10 minutes; strain, discarding cloves and onion.

Return sauce to pan. Stir together 1 tablespoon *each* **cornstarch** and **water** until smooth; stir into sauce and cook, stirring, until it boils and thickens. Stir in cherries, ¼ teaspoon **grated lemon peel,** and 1 tablespoon **lemon juice.**

Game Hens with Papaya and Curry Pilaf

⏱ *Thaw frozen birds. Preparation time: 15 minutes. Cooking time: 1 hour*

Curried pilaf bakes alongside the chutney basted game hens. Garnish the hens with papaya slices heated briefly in the game hen juices.

   2 **Rock Cornish game hens (16 to 20 oz. e*ach*)**
      Salt and pepper
   2 **tablespoons butter or margarine, melted**
   1 **teaspoon curry powder**
      Curry pilaf (recipe follows)
   3 **tablespoons Major Grey's chutney, finely chopped**
   2 **tablespoons lime juice**
   1 **large (or 2 small) papaya**
      Lime wedges

Thaw hens as directed on package (set giblets aside for other uses); rinse hens and pat dry. Sprinkle inside cavities with salt and pepper. Place hens slightly apart, breast sides up, in a roasting pan. Combine butter and curry; brush over hens, using it all. Roast, uncovered, in a 350° oven for about 1 hour or until leg joints move easily. Meanwhile, prepare pilaf and set into oven alongside hens.

After 30 minutes' roasting, remove hens from oven, stir chutney and lime juice into pan drippings, and baste hens with mixture. Return to oven and continue baking, basting hens with drippings 2 or 3 times.

Remove hens from pan and arrange on a warm serving plate; keep warm. Peel papaya, cut in half, and discard seeds. Cut in ½-inch-thick slices. Turn papaya in pan drippings, then return to oven until papaya is heated through (about 5 minutes). Remove papaya from oven and arrange around hens; spoon pan juices over top. Garnish with lime wedges and serve with curry pilaf.

(Continued on next page)

Curry pilaf. In a wide frying pan over medium heat, melt 2 tablespoons **butter** or margarine. Stir in 1 small **onion,** chopped; 1 clove **garlic,** minced or pressed; and 1 teaspoon **curry powder.** Cook, stirring, over medium heat, for about 2 minutes. Add 1 cup **long-grain rice;** cook, stirring, for about 5 minutes. Add 2¼ cups **regular-strength chicken broth** (or 3 chicken bouillon cubes mixed with 2¼ cups water) and ½ teaspoon **salt.** Transfer to a 1½ to 2-quart baking dish. Cover and bake in a 350° oven for 30 to 45 minutes or until rice is tender to bite and liquid is absorbed.

Turkey Schnitzel

🕐 *Preparation time: 10 minutes. Marinating time: 30 minutes. Cooking time: 6 minutes*

Some markets slice and package uncooked turkey breast meat so that it can be purchased easily in amounts just right for two. Or you can purchase a half or whole breast, slice the meat for this recipe, then roast or poach the remainder to use in sandwiches, salads, and casseroles.

- 4 turkey breast slices, cut about ½ inch thick (about ¾ lb. total)
- 2 tablespoons lemon juice
- ¼ cup olive oil or salad oil
- ⅛ teaspoon *each* salt and pepper
- ⅓ cup *each* all-purpose flour and grated Parmesan cheese
- 2 to 3 tablespoons butter or margarine

Place meat between 2 sheets of wax paper or plastic wrap and pound ¼ inch thick with smooth side of a mallet. Mix together lemon juice, oil, salt, and pepper. Place pounded turkey in a shallow pan and pour over lemon juice mixture; cover and refrigerate at least 30 minutes or as long as overnight.

Drain liquid from turkey. Mix together flour and Parmesan cheese; coat turkey generously with mixture and shake off excess. Heat 2 tablespoons of the butter in a wide frying pan over medium-high heat. Quickly cook turkey slices until lightly browned on both sides (3 to 5 minutes per side), adding more butter if needed.

Braised Turkey Drumsticks

🕐 *Preparation time: 10 minutes. Cooking time: 2 hours and 15 minutes*

Cooked to moist tenderness in a wine and broth mixture with celery and carrots, these turkey legs are good with baked potatoes and mixed sweet pickles. You'll want to make this dish when you have a little time—it takes about 2 hours to cook.

- 2 tablespoons butter or margarine
- 2 small turkey legs (1½ to 1¾ lb. total)
- 1 small clove garlic, minced or pressed
- 1 medium-size onion, sliced and separated into rings
- 1 large stalk celery, thinly sliced diagonally
- 2 medium-size carrots, thinly sliced diagonally
- ¼ cup *each* regular-strength chicken broth and dry white wine (or ½ cup broth)
- ½ teaspoon seasoned salt
  Dash pepper
  Chopped parsley

Melt butter in a wide frying pan over medium-high heat. Add turkey and cook until browned on all sides. Add garlic, onion, celery, and carrots; cook until onion is limp. Stir in chicken broth, wine, seasoned salt, and pepper. Bring to a boil, reduce heat, cover tightly, and simmer 2 hours or until turkey is very tender when pierced.

With a slotted spoon, remove turkey and vegetables to a warm serving dish. Over high heat, boil pan juices to reduce by about ⅓; pour over turkey. Sprinkle with parsley.

Turkey and Fried Rice

🕐 *Cook rice ahead. Preparation time: 10 minutes. Cooking time: 10 minutes*

When you have cooked turkey at hand, this dish can be put together quickly. With a green salad, it makes a satisfying supper. Plan to cook the rice in advance.

- 2 tablespoons salad oil
- ¼ cup *each* chopped onion and green bell pepper
- 1 cup cold cooked rice
- 1 clove garlic, minced or pressed
  About 1½ cups thinly sliced celery, carrots, mushrooms, water chestnuts, or zucchini
- 1½ cups cooked turkey cut in bite-size pieces
- 1 egg, beaten
- 1 tablespoon soy sauce
- 4 cherry tomatoes, quartered
  Chopped green onion or parsley

Heat oil in a wide frying pan or wok over medium-high heat; add onion and pepper and cook, stirring, until onion is limp. Sprinkle in rice and garlic and stir constantly until rice is evenly coated with oil. Add vegetables and cook, stirring, for 2 to 4 minutes (vegetables should be tender crisp). Stir in meat to heat throughly, then push mixture to sides of pan. Pour in egg and cook until just set; add soy and tomatoes and mix into rice along with egg. Turn into a serving dish. Sprinkle with green onion or parsley.

SEAFOOD

Seafood has all kinds of advantages. High in nutrition, it is low in calories and fat. It has little waste and is easily purchased in quantities just right for one or two. It cooks quickly—indeed, you should be careful not to overcook, and a good rule with fish is to allow 10 minutes cooking time per inch of thickness.

But seafood's greatest attribute is its wonderful taste, followed closely by its versatility. In this chapter are recipes for fish blanketed in delicate sauces, stir-fried teriyaki-style, sautéed with butter and almonds, baked in casseroles, simmered in stews. All are surprisingly quick to prepare and marvelous to eat.

Our recipes give quantities, but to guide you in general buying of seafood, we offer the following:

When you buy boneless fillets or steaks, allow ¾ to 1 pound for two people; small whole fish such as trout, about 1½ pounds. For shrimp in the shell, about a pound for two servings; out of shell, about ¾ pound. Scallops or crab out of shell, about ¾ pound for two people; for crab in shell, plan on 2 to 3 pounds crab. Sixteen to 24 clams or oysters make a meal for two.

Barbecued Salmon Fillet

🕐 *Heat coals: 35 minutes. Preparation time: 10 minutes. Cooking time: 10 minutes per inch of fish thickness*

Fresh salmon fillets are delicious barbecued with a baste of butter, wine, lemon juice, and soy sauce. Add corn-on-the-cob and juicy sliced tomatoes to complete this simple meal.

> ¾ to 1-pound salmon fillet
> 2 tablespoons butter or margarine, melted
> ¼ cup rosé or dry white wine
> 2 tablespoons *each* lemon juice and soy sauce
> Parsley and lemon wedges

Ignite coals about 35 minutes before you intend to begin cooking (you will need about 20 to 30 long-burning briquets). When coals are covered with gray ash, arrange in a single layer to underlie area being used on grill. Knock ash off coals. Adjust grill to 4 to 6 inches above low-glowing coals. Cut heavy-duty foil the same size as fish fillet. Place fillet, skin side down, on foil.

Combine butter, wine, lemon juice, and soy sauce. Place fish on grill, foil side down, and brush generously with butter sauce. Cover barbecue with its hood (or fashion a hood out of heavy-duty foil and place on grill to enclose fish). Cook, basting with butter sauce about every 5 minutes, until fish flakes readily when prodded in thickest portion with a fork (allow about 10 minutes cooking time for each inch of thickness).

To serve, slide fish, still on foil, onto a serving plate or board. Garnish with parsley and lemon. Slice fish to the skin and lift each serving away from skin. Reheat any remaining butter sauce and pass at table to serve over fish.

Salmon Ramekins with Hollandaise

🕐 *Preparation time: 10 minutes. Cooking time: 15 minutes*

Attractively presented in individual ramekins, this salmon with hollandaise is made with ingredients that are easily kept on hand in cupboard and freezer. You can put it together on a moment's notice.

> 1 package (9 or 10 oz.) frozen Italian green beans
> Boiling salted water
> 1 can (about 8 oz.) salmon, drained
> 1 can (6 oz.) hollandaise sauce or ¾ cup homemade hollandaise
> ¼ teaspoon grated lemon peel
> ⅛ teaspoon tarragon, crumbled
> 2 tablespoons sliced or slivered blanched almonds

(Continued on next page)

Cook beans as directed on the package in boiling salted water until just tender; drain. Break salmon into large chunks, remove and discard bones and skin. Lightly butter two individual ramekins (1 to 1½ cups each) and spoon in beans and salmon chunks. Mix together hollandaise, lemon peel, and tarragon; spoon equal amounts of sauce over salmon and beans. Sprinkle with almonds. Bake in a 350° oven for about 15 minutes or until hot through.

Fillet of Sole Bonne Femme

🕐 *Preparation time: 10 minutes. Cooking time: 20 minutes*

Delicately flavored sole cooked in white wine and cream makes a classic fish dish for two. Serve it with buttered green beans or lightly cooked zucchini.

- **4 sole fillets (¾ to 1 lb. total)**
  Salt and pepper
- **1 green onion, sliced (include some green tops)**
- **½ lemon, thinly sliced**
- **⅓ cup dry white wine**
  Water
- **2 tablespoons butter or margarine**
- **¼ pound mushrooms, sliced**
- **2 teaspoons all-purpose flour**
- **1 egg yolk**
- **2 tablespoons whipping cream**
  Chopped parsley and lemon wedges

Sprinkle sole lightly with salt and pepper. Fold fillets crosswise and place in a greased 8-inch-square baking pan. Top with onion and lemon slices; pour wine over all. Cover and bake in a 400° oven for 15 to 20 minutes or until fish flakes easily when prodded in thickest portion with a fork. Remove from oven; discard lemon slices. Drain pan liquid into a measuring cup; add water, if necessary, to make ½ cup. Keep sole warm.

Melt butter in a small pan over medium-high heat; add mushrooms and cook until lightly browned. Stir in flour until bubbly. Gradually add cooking liquid from fish and cook, stirring constantly, until thickened. In a bowl, combine egg yolk with cream and beat; stir in a little of the hot liquid from mushrooms. Add egg mixture to mushroom sauce in pan and cook, stirring constantly, until thickened.

Lift sole onto a warm serving dish. Blend a little of the liquid that collected in fish pan into mushroom sauce to thin it slightly, if needed. Spoon sauce over fish. Serve immediately, garnished with chopped parsley and lemon wedges.

Red Snapper Stew

🕐 *Preparation time (cooking included): 20 minutes*

Red snapper and vegetables simmer in a savory tomato broth, ready to serve in minutes with French bread for dipping into the broth.

- **3 tablespoons olive oil or salad oil**
- **1 clove garlic, minced or pressed**
- **1 large onion, chopped**
- **1 green pepper, seeded and chopped**
- **1 can (8 oz.) tomatoes**
- **1 can (12 oz.) tomato juice**
- **½ teaspoon salt**
- **¼ cup dry white wine (or 1 tablespoon lemon juice and 3 tablespoons water)**
- **½ teaspoon oregano leaves**
- **1 teaspoon Worcestershire**
- **1 pound boned and skinned red snapper or other rockfish, cut in 1½-inch cubes**

In a 3 to 4-quart pan, heat oil over medium heat. Add garlic, onion, and green pepper; cook, stirring occasionally, until onion is limp. Add tomatoes (break them up with a spoon) and their liquid. Stir in tomato juice, salt, wine, oregano, and Worcestershire; bring to a boil. Add red snapper, then cover and simmer, stirring occasionally, until fish flakes easily when prodded with a fork (about 8 minutes).

Trout with Almonds

🕐 *Preparation time: 5 minutes. Cooking time: 10 minutes per inch of fish thickness*

Butter-toasted almonds are sprinkled over sautéed trout just before serving. (See photograph on facing page.)

- **4 tablespoons butter or margarine**
- **4 to 8 tablespoons sliced almonds**
- **2 medium-size trout (about ½ lb. each)**
  Salt (optional)
- **1 tablespoon each lemon juice and chopped parsley**

In a wide frying pan over medium heat, melt 2 tablespoons of the butter and add almonds. Cook, stirring, until nuts are toasted golden. Pour nuts and butter from pan into a container and set aside.

(Continued on page 60)

BUTTER-TOASTED ALMOND SLIVERS blanket trout quickly sautéed at the last minute (recipe above). Plan on one or two trout per person for this meal in minutes.

In same pan, melt remaining 2 tablespoons butter over medium-high heat and add fish. Cook until browned lightly on 1 side. Add more butter, if needed, and turn fish over with a wide spatula. Cook second side until lightly browned and fish flakes readily when prodded with a fork in thickest portion (allow 10 minutes—5 minutes each side—total cooking time for each 1 inch of thickness). Sprinkle fish lightly with salt, if desired.

Sprinkle reserved almonds on fish, then spoon over lemon juice and parsley.

Tuna Turnover

🕐 *Preparation time: 20 minutes. Cooking time: 20 minutes*

Puffy pastry is filled with a crunchy tuna salad mixture to make one big turnover. While it bakes, sip hot beef-flavored tomato cocktail topped with freshly ground pepper and lime juice. Count on 1 to 1½ cups for each of you.

> **Pastry for single-crust 9-inch pie**
> **2 tablespoons butter or margarine, at room temperature**
> **1 can (6½ oz.) chunk-style tuna, well drained**
> **⅓ cup *each* thinly sliced green onion and celery**
> **⅓ cup chopped dry roasted peanuts**
> **⅓ cup sour cream**
> **1 teaspoon lemon juice**
> **½ teaspoon dill weed**
> **1 red or green bell pepper, seeded and cut in rings**
> **Dill pickle slices**

Prepare your favorite pie pastry or use a packaged mix. Roll out dough on a lightly floured board into a 12-inch circle. Spread evenly with butter.

Combine tuna, onion, celery, peanuts, sour cream, lemon juice, and dill weed; spread mixture over half the dough to about 1 inch from edge. Fold unfilled half over the tuna mixture and crimp edges with tines of a fork to seal in filling.

With a wide spatula, transfer to an ungreased baking sheet; slash top in 2 or 3 places. Bake in a 425° oven, uncovered, for about 20 minutes or until golden brown. Remove to serving platter; garnish with pepper rings and dill pickles. Serve at once.

Tuna Pot Pie

🕐 *Preparation time: 15 minutes. Cooking time: 30 minutes*

Refrigerated biscuits top a tempting tuna pie filled with baby carrots and potato slices. For the bottom

"crust" you mash slices of potatoes into an even layer before filling. Serve pot pie with a salad of romaine leaves mixed with mandarin oranges and bean sprouts.

> **1 tablespoon butter or margarine**
> **1 small onion, chopped**
> **1 medium-size potato, peeled and cut in ¼-inch slices**
> **1 cup water**
> **2 teaspoons chicken stock base**
> **1 package (10 oz.) frozen baby carrots or sliced carrots and peas, thawed**
> **¼ teaspoon *each* dill weed, salt, and liquid hot pepper seasoning**
> **1 tablespoon chopped parsley**
> **1 can (7 oz.) solid pack tuna, drained**
> **1 small package (4½ oz.) refrigerated biscuits**

Melt butter in a pan over medium heat. Add onion and cook, stirring, until limp. Add potato, water, and chicken stock base; cook, covered, until potato is almost tender (about 8 minutes). Stir in carrots, cover, and cook for 2 or 3 minutes. Remove from heat and stir in dill, salt, hot pepper seasoning, and parsley; gently mix in tuna, breaking it apart in large chunks.

Pick out 2 large slices of the potato and put in bottom of a 1-quart casserole; mash with a fork, spreading evenly over bottom of casserole. Pour remaining tuna mixture into casserole. Arrange 3 to 6 of the biscuits on top. (Place any remaining biscuits in another pan to bake with the casserole.)

Bake casserole, uncovered, in a 400° oven until biscuits are well browned and mixture is bubbly (about 20 minutes).

juice, and onion. Spoon sauce over fish and spinach. Sprinkle with remaining 3 tablespoons cheese.

Bake, uncovered, in a 425° oven for about 15 minutes or until bubbly and lightly browned. Garnish with chopped parsley.

Scampi

⏱ *Preparation time: 10 minutes. Cooking time: 6 minutes*

For a quick version of the heady garlic-flavored scampi served in many Italian restaurants, try these shrimp sautéed with lemon juice and garlic. Rice makes a good accompaniment.

   6 tablespoons butter or margarine
   1 tablespoon minced green onion
   1 tablespoon olive oil or salad oil
   4 to 5 cloves garlic, minced or pressed
   2 teaspoons lemon juice
   ¼ teaspoon salt
      About ¾ pound medium-size shrimp, shelled (but tails intact) and deveined
   ¼ teaspoon grated lemon peel
   2 tablespoons minced parsley
      Dash liquid hot pepper seasoning
      Lemon wedges

Melt butter in a wide frying pan over medium heat. Stir in onion, oil, garlic, lemon juice, and salt; cook until bubbly. Add shrimp to pan and cook, stirring occasionally, until shrimp turn pink (about 5 minutes). Stir in lemon peel, parsley, and hot pepper seasoning; turn into serving dish. Garnish with lemon wedges to squeeze over each serving.

Scampi for one. Use 2 tablespoons **butter** or margarine; 1½ teaspoons minced **green onion;** 1½ teaspoons **olive oil** or salad oil; 2 cloves **garlic,** minced or pressed; 1 teaspoon **lemon juice;** ⅛ teaspoon **salt;** 6 ounces **shrimp;** ⅛ teaspoon grated **lemon peel;** 1 tablespoon minced **parsley;** and a dash of **liquid hot pepper seasoning.**

Sole Florentine

⏱ *Preparation time: 15 minutes. Cooking time: 15 minutes*

Rolled fillets of sole bake in a creamy sauce atop a bed of spinach. Use a shallow baking dish or individual ramekins.

   4 sole fillets (¾ to 1 lb. total)
   1 bottle (8 oz.) clam juice
   1 package (10 oz.) frozen chopped spinach, thawed
   4 tablespoons grated Parmesan cheese
   2 tablespoons butter or margarine
   2 tablespoons all-purpose flour
   ⅔ cup milk
   ⅛ teaspoon ground nutmeg
   ¼ teaspoon dry mustard
   1 tablespoon *each* lemon juice and instant minced onion
      Chopped parsley

Loosely roll each fillet and secure with a pick. In a pan bring clam juice to a boil; set in sole, cover, and simmer for 3 to 5 minutes or until opaque white. Remove fish and drain. Boil clam juice, uncovered, until reduced to ½ cup; pour into cup and set aside.

Meanwhile, drain spinach well; distribute over bottom of a shallow 1-quart baking dish or 2 individual ramekins. Sprinkle evenly with 1 tablespoon of the Parmesan. Remove picks and arrange fish on spinach. Melt butter in pan over medium heat, blend in flour, and cook, stirring, until bubbly. Remove from heat and gradually stir in milk and clam juice; cook and stir until thickened. Add nutmeg, mustard, lemon

Shrimp and Mushroom Ramekins

⏱ *Preparation time: 10 minutes. Cooking time: 22 minutes*

Individual servings of cheese-blanketed shrimp bake with golden mushroom slices in a rich cream sauce while you prepare an accompanying green vegetable such as zucchini, broccoli, or green beans. Consider a light dessert of caramel custard (page 76).

(Continued on page 63)

4 tablespoons butter or margarine
¾ pound medium-size shrimp, shelled and deveined
¼ pound mushrooms, sliced
2 tablespoons chopped green onion
2 tablespoons all-purpose flour
⅛ teaspoon Dijon mustard
⅓ cup regular-strength chicken broth
¼ cup whipping cream
2 tablespoons dry sherry
   Salt and pepper
½ cup shredded Swiss cheese

Melt 2 tablespoons of the butter in a frying pan over medium heat; add shrimp and cook, stirring often, until shrimp turn pink (about 5 minutes). Transfer shrimp to 2 individual baking dishes.

To pan, add remaining 2 tablespoons butter, mushrooms, and green onion. Cook over medium heat, stirring, until mushrooms are golden brown; sprinkle in flour and cook until bubbly. Gradually stir in mustard, broth, and cream. Cook, stirring, until thickened and bubbly. Stir in sherry and salt and pepper to taste; spoon evenly over shrimp, and sprinkle with cheese. Bake, uncovered, in a 325° oven for 10 to 15 minutes or until hot through and cheese is melted.

Drizzle remaining butter evenly over crumbs. Place baking dish on oven rack near top of oven. Bake, uncovered, in a 400° oven until crumbs on top are well browned (12 to 15 minutes). Serve immediately.

Shrimp-Scallop Teriyaki

⏱ *Preparation time: 15 minutes. Marinating time: 30 minutes. Cooking time: 5 minutes*

The luxury of stir-frying is that you can add ingredients to your heart's content. The photograph on page 62 suggests possibilities for varying this recipe with more vegetables—the quantity depends on your appetite. If you do add vegetables beyond what the recipe calls for, do so just before you add the seafood, stir-frying each additional quarter-pound of sliced vegetables in 1 to 2 more tablespoons of oil until just tender-crisp. (See photograph on facing page.)

4 tablespoons prepared teriyaki sauce
3 tablespoons dry sherry
1½ teaspoons finely chopped fresh ginger or ½ teaspoon ground ginger
2 cloves garlic, minced or pressed
1½ teaspoons cornstarch
½ pound medium-size shrimp, shelled and deveined
½ pound scallops, well rinsed
4 tablespoons peanut oil or salad oil
¼ pound edible-pod peas or 1 package (6 oz.) frozen pod peas, thawed and drained
½ pound mushrooms, sliced
5 green onions, cut in 2-inch lengths

Mix teriyaki sauce, sherry, ginger, garlic, and cornstarch in a deep container and add shrimp and scallops. Cover and refrigerate for at least ½ hour.

When ready to cook, assemble remaining ingredients so that you can reach them quickly. Pour 2 tablespoons of the oil into a wok or frying pan over high heat; when oil is hot, add peas and cook, stirring rapidly, until peas are bright green. Remove peas and set aside. Add remaining 2 tablespoons oil, heat again, and quickly stir and fry mushrooms. Pour in shrimp and scallops with their liquid; add onion and cook, stirring, over high heat until shrimp turn pink. Stir in reserved pod peas, remove from heat, and serve.

Oven-fried Oysters

⏱ *Preparation time: 10 minutes. Cooking time: 12 minutes*

Rich, buttery, and crisply crusted, these baked oysters make a satisfying main dish accompanied by peas tossed with sliced celery lightly sautéed in butter. Serve a dessert of mint ice cream and cookies.

About 16 saltine crackers
1 jar (10 oz.) small or medium-size oysters
6 tablespoons butter or margarine, melted
   Salt and pepper

Crush enough crackers to make ¾ cup fine crumbs. Spread ½ of the crumbs over bottom of a buttered 8 to 9-inch square baking dish. Drain oysters, then dip them into melted butter to coat well. Arrange oysters in a single layer over crumbs. Sprinkle lightly with salt and pepper to taste. Top with remaining crumbs.

IN A WOK, shrimp and scallops stir-fry quickly after marinating in teriyaki sauce (recipe at right). Add as many different sliced vegetables as your appetite desires.

For Color & Verve, Think Vegetables

There's nothing like vegetables for adding color, texture, and taste—not to mention nutrition—to a meal. Cooked to just the right degree of doneness, they become the perfect partner for an entrée.

And because we know there will be times when you'll just want to steam your vegetables or cook them in a small amount of boiling water, we've included a chart that lists a number of favorite vegetables and the amount to buy when you're cooking for two.

You can figure quantities when you're buying fresh vegetables for one or two when you're dealing with one-apiece vegetables (maybe two-apiece, depending on your appetite) such as tomatoes, corn on the cob, potatoes, or artichokes. With others, though, you may need some guidance.

The trick is to approximate the amount of waste involved. Most fresh vegetables fall into one of two categories—those that, when purchased, are about half waste, and those with almost no waste. A general rule is that you'll need about a quarter-pound of *edible* vegetable per serving.

The recipes on these pages tell you how much to buy for two servings of these specific dishes. But when you just want to boil or steam a vegetable for simple presentation, use the following buying guide.

Vegetable	To Serve Two, Buy This Amount
Asparagus	1 pound
Beans, green or yellow wax	½ pound
Broccoli	⅔ to 1 pound
Brussels sprouts	½ pound
Carrots	½ pound
Mushrooms	½ pound
Parsnips	½ pound
Peas in shells	1 pound
Peas, edible pod	½ pound
Spinach	½ to ⅔ pound
Squash, summer (crookneck, patty pan, zucchini)	½ pound
Squash, winter (acorn, banana, butternut, Hubbard)	⅔ pound
Turnips	½ pound

Asparagus in Wine

Asparagus, cooked just until tender-crisp, is treated to a butter and wine sauce, then a dusting of Parmesan cheese. Special though it is, it takes only minutes.

- **1 pound asparagus**
  Salted water
- **2 tablespoons butter or margarine**
- **2 tablespoons dry white wine**
  Salt and white pepper
- **3 tablespoons shredded Parmesan cheese**

Snap off and discard tough ends from asparagus; wash asparagus. In a wide frying pan, bring ½ inch salted water to a boil. Add asparagus, cover, and cook over medium heat until tender-crisp when pierced (5 to 7 minutes). Drain well and turn into a shallow 3 to 4-cup casserole.

Melt butter in frying pan over high heat; add wine and cook, uncovered, until reduced by about half. Pour butter-wine sauce over asparagus. Sprinkle with salt and pepper to taste, then with cheese. Place under broiler, 2 to 3 inches from heat, until cheese melts (about 2 minutes).

Gingered Carrots with Sesame

The sweetness of carrots comes forth when they cook, and the freshness of ginger amplifies this sweetness. Garnish the carrot sticks with sesame seeds toasted to a nutlike flavor. (See photograph on page 31.)

- **1 tablespoon sesame seeds**
- **6 medium-size carrots**
- **¼ cup boiling salted water**
- **2 tablespoons butter or margarine**
- **1½ teaspoons minced candied ginger or grated fresh ginger, or ¾ teaspoon ground ginger**
  Chopped parsley

Toast sesame seeds in a frying pan over medium heat until golden, stirring frequently. Set aside.

Peel carrots and cut into slender sticks about 3 inches long. Place in a pan with boiling salted water. Cover and cook over medium heat until just tender (8 to 10 minutes); drain. Add butter and ginger and cook, stirring, until carrots are glazed. To serve, sprinkle with reserved toasted sesame seeds and parsley.

Posh Squash

Bright yellow crookneck squash makes a colorful casserole topped with cheese. It is especially appealing with barbecued meats.

About ¾ pound crookneck squash
Boiling salted water
1 **egg**
⅓ **cup mayonnaise**
¼ **cup finely chopped onion**
2 **tablespoons chopped green pepper**
⅛ **teaspoon thyme leaves**
Salt and pepper
⅓ **cup grated Parmesan cheese**
½ **tablespoon butter or margarine**

Cut off and discard stem and blossom ends from squash; scrub squash but do not peel. Cut into ½-inch-thick slices and cook, covered, in a small amount of boiling salted water until just tender when pierced (3 to 5 minutes), drain well and set aside.

Beat egg, then blend in mayonnaise, onion, green pepper, and thyme. Stir in squash and add salt and pepper to taste.

Spoon mixture into a greased shallow 1-quart casserole; sprinkle evenly with cheese and dot with butter. Cover and chill if made ahead. Bake, uncovered, in a 375° oven for 20 minutes (25 minutes if refrigerated) or until puffed and lightly browned.

Baked Stuffed Eggplant

A Turkish delight, baked eggplant is well suited for lamb dishes. For a Middle-Eastern touch, serve unflavored yogurt to spoon over both eggplant and accompanying meat. The eggplant takes time to bake, but you can make it ahead and then serve it at room temperature. (See photograph on page 39.)

1 **small eggplant (about ¾ lb.)**
Salt
3 **tablespoons olive oil or salad oil**
1 **medium-size onion, thinly sliced**
2 **small cloves garlic, minced or pressed**
¼ **cup minced parsley**
½ **teaspoon sugar**
¾ **teaspoon salt**
1 **large tomato, peeled, seeded, and diced**
2 **tablespoons pine nuts**

Cut eggplant in half lengthwise and scoop out center, leaving a firm ½-inch-thick shell; reserve pulp.

Sprinkle shells lightly with salt. Use 1 tablespoon of the oil to grease a shallow baking pan; arrange eggplant in pan, skin side down.

Place remaining 2 tablespoons oil in a wide frying pan over medium-high heat; add onion and cook until limp. Stir in about 1 cup reserved eggplant pulp (diced), garlic, parsley, sugar, the ¾ teaspoon salt, and tomato. Evenly distribute filling in eggplant shells.

Place pine nuts on a shallow rimmed baking sheet. Bake in a 350° oven for 8 to 10 minutes or until toasted. Set aside.

Cover eggplant pan with foil and bake in a 350° oven for about 1 hour or until tender. Sprinkle with toasted pine nuts and serve hot or at room temperature.

Spinach Soufflé-stuffed Mushrooms

Bright green puffs of spinach soufflé nestle in large mushroom caps for a vegetable side dish that is good-tasting and elegant. (See photograph on page 31.)

6 **mushrooms, each at least 2 inches in diameter**
2 **tablespoons butter or margarine**
½ **pound spinach**
Dash of garlic powder
1 **egg**
1 **tablespoon all-purpose flour**
About 2 tablespoons grated Parmesan cheese

Remove stems from mushrooms; reserve for other uses. Melt 1 tablespoon of the butter in a wide frying pan over medium heat. Turn mushroom caps over in butter and arrange in a greased baking pan, cup side up; set aside.

Remove stems from spinach; wash leaves well. Add spinach, with water that clings to leaves, to frying pan; cook over medium heat until wilted (about 3 minutes). Press out all liquid. Whirl garlic powder and egg in a blender until egg is frothy; add spinach and whirl until smooth.

Melt remaining 1 tablespoon butter in frying pan, add flour, and cook, stirring, until bubbly; remove from heat and stir in spinach mixture.

Spoon equal amounts of spinach mixture into each mushroom cap. Sprinkle evenly with Parmesan cheese. Bake, uncovered, in a 400° oven for 10 to 15 minutes or until cheese is golden and soufflé puffy. Serve immediately.

Crab Vermouth

🕐 *Preparation time: 10 minutes. Cooking time: 20 minutes.*

Crab's delicate flavor needs only a simple presentation to be at its best. Here it is enhanced by a light but well-seasoned broth with overtones of dry vermouth and garlic. It is so easy to make—just heat cooked cracked crab in the broth and ladle it into serving bowls. Serve with crusty French bread for dunking.

- ¼ cup butter or margarine
- 1 tablespoon cornstarch (optional)
- 1 cup regular-strength chicken broth
- ½ cup dry vermouth
- 1 tablespoon chopped parsley
- 2 cloves garlic, minced or pressed
- 1½ teaspoons *each* soy sauce and lemon juice
- ½ teaspoon sugar
- 1 large (about 2 lbs.) cooked crab, cleaned and cracked
- 2 tablespoons dry vermouth
  Hot French bread

Melt butter in a wide frying pan over medium heat. If you want a slightly thickened broth, remove butter from heat and blend in cornstarch.

Gradually stir in chicken broth and the ½ cup dry vermouth. Add parsley, garlic, soy sauce, lemon juice, and sugar. Bring to a boil, reduce heat, cover, and simmer for 10 minutes.

To hot broth, add crab; cover and simmer until crab is heated through (about 10 minutes). Pour the 2 tablespoons dry vermouth over crab.

Ladle into shallow bowls. Serve with French bread for dunking.

Spaghetti with Clam Sauce

🕐 *Preparation time: 10 minutes. Cooking time: 18 minutes.*

Fresh clams lace the spaghetti sauce flavored with garlic, white wine, and plenty of parsley. Add garlic bread or bread sticks and a salad with marinated artichoke hearts for a complete meal.

- 16 fresh clams in the shell, well scrubbed
- ½ cup water
- 1 tablespoon butter or margarine
- ¼ pound spaghetti
- 2 cloves garlic, minced or pressed
- 2 shallots, minced
- ½ cup dry white wine
- 1 tablespoon cornstarch blended with 1 tablespoon water
- ¼ cup minced parsley

Place clams in a pot that they fill about halfway. Add water, cover, and simmer for about 8 minutes or until shells open; discard any unopened clams. Lift pan from heat and remove clams from their shells. Return clams to liquid in pan; discard shells.

Prepare spaghetti according to package directions.

Melt butter in a wide frying pan over medium-low heat. Add garlic and shallots and cook, uncovered, until limp but not brown (3 to 4 minutes). Add wine and clam liquid; simmer, uncovered, for about 5 minutes to blend flavors. Add cornstarch mixture and cook, stirring constantly, until bubbling. Remove from heat, pour in clams and any remaining liquid, then stir in parsley.

Drain spaghetti, mix in clam sauce, and serve at once.

Clams Bordelaise

🕐 *Cook rice ahead. Preparation time: 10 minutes. Cooking time: 7 minutes*

Named for the white Bordeaux wine originally used to flavor the broth, clams bordelaise can be made with any dry white wine—or with lemon juice. Serve the clams, rice, and broth in a broad shallow soup bowl with a spoon and fork. A simple salad, classic bread sticks, and dry white wine provide a French-style meal. (See photograph on facing page.)

- 2 tablespoons butter or margarine
- 2 tablespoons finely chopped parsley
- 1 clove garlic, minced or pressed
  About 1 cup regular-strength chicken broth
- ½ cup dry white wine (or 2 tablespoons lemon juice with ⅓ cup regular-strength chicken broth)
- 16 fresh clams in the shell, well scrubbed
- 1 cup hot cooked rice

Melt butter in a 3-quart pan over medium heat. Add parsley and garlic and cook for 1 to 2 minutes. Pour in chicken broth and wine and bring to a boil. Add clams, cover, and cook over medium heat until clams open (5 to 10 minutes), adding more broth, if desired. Discard any unopened clams. To serve, spoon some of the hot rice into wide shallow bowls, arrange opened clams in each, then pour over broth and serve.

FIRESIDE DINNER FOR TWO includes steamed clams, crunchy sesame seed bread sticks, and chilled white wine. Clams cook in a flavorful broth of wine and garlic laden with rice in just a matter of minutes (recipe above). Accompany with grapes or other fruit.

EGGS & CHEESE

Eggs are a food for all seasons—and for all hours of the day and night. What's more, they usually are present in even the most barren refrigerator, ready for any presentation from simple to elegant.

Cheese is a good partner for eggs in spur-of-the-moment meals. It, too, is convenient to keep on hand, and it is available in impressive variety.

Put the two together according to the recipes that follow, and you get quiches, soufflés, egg enchiladas, omelets—all perfect answers when you're looking for something light and lovely to cook.

Cheese Soufflé

Preparation time: 10 minutes. Cooking time: 18 minutes

A soufflé, the aristocrat of the egg family, can be assembled in minutes. You should be ready to sit down and eat as soon as it's out of the oven, though it will hold in the oven for about 5 minutes before falling. Bake it in individual soufflé dishes or one larger dish. Serve a favorite salad while the soufflé bakes, then accompany your masterpiece with a green vegetable, such as broccoli spears.

  1 tablespoon butter or margarine
  1 tablespoon all-purpose flour
 ⅓ cup milk
    Dash of cayenne pepper
 ⅛ teaspoon dry mustard
 ¾ cup shredded sharp Cheddar cheese
  2 tablespoons grated Parmesan cheese
  2 eggs, separated

In a pan over medium heat, melt butter, stir in flour, and cook, stirring, until bubbly. Remove from heat and gradually stir in milk; add cayenne and mustard. Cook, stirring, until thick. Add Cheddar cheese and 1 tablespoon of the Parmesan; stir over heat until cheese melts. Remove cheese mixture from heat and beat in egg yolks. Beat egg whites until they hold distinct but moist peaks; carefully fold into cheese mixture.

Butter well a 3 to 4-cup soufflé dish or 2 individual 1¼-cup soufflé dishes; coat inside with remaining 1 tablespoon Parmesan cheese. Pour in soufflé mixture and with the tip of a knife, draw a circle on top surface about 1 inch inside rim. Bake in a 350° oven until soufflé feels firm when lightly tapped and crack looks fairly dry (about 18 to 20 minutes for a 1-quart dish, 12 to 15 minutes for individual dishes).

Onion Soufflé

Preparation time: 15 minutes. Cooking time: 18 minutes

Onions, used discreetly, give a mildly robust flavor to a soufflé that is good with any simply cooked meat or fish. Baked in individual soufflé dishes, it would add special flair to a patio supper featuring barbecued steaks.

  2 tablespoons butter or margarine
  1 medium-size onion, chopped
1½ tablespoons all-purpose flour
 ¼ teaspoon salt
    Dash of thyme leaves, crumbled
    Dash of white pepper
 ⅓ cup milk
  3 eggs, separated

Melt butter in a pan over medium heat; add onion and cook until soft and lightly browned. Stir in flour, salt, thyme, and pepper and cook until bubbly. Remove from heat and gradually stir in milk. Cook, stirring, until very thick. Whirl in blender or food processor until smooth.

Return sauce to pan and heat to simmering, stirring. Remove from heat and beat in egg yolks. Heat and stir for a few seconds or until thick again; remove from heat. Whip egg whites until they hold short, distinct, moist peaks. Fold half the whites thoroughly into sauce, then fold in remaining whites.

Pour into well-buttered individual 1¼-cup soufflé dishes or a 3 to 4-cup soufflé dish. Bake in a 375° oven for about 18 to 20 minutes or until brown. Serve immediately.

Baked Egg and Tomato Ramekins

Preparation time: 5 minutes. Cooking time: 35 minutes

The affinity of eggs and tomatoes is evident in this tempting egg dish baked in individual casseroles. Serve them for a leisurely weekend brunch with sausage links and toasted English muffins.

> 1 can (about 14 oz.) stewed tomatoes, drained
> 2 tablespoons butter or margarine
> ½ cup sliced green onion
> ¼ pound mushrooms, sliced
> 1 tablespoon all-purpose flour
> ¼ teaspoon *each* dry basil and garlic salt
> Dash *each* pepper and sugar
> 3 tablespoons grated Parmesan cheese
> 2 eggs
> Chopped parsley

With a spoon, press tomatoes gently in a wire strainer to remove remaining liquid (save for other uses); set tomatoes aside.

In a pan, melt 1 tablespoon of the butter. Add onion and mushrooms. Cook, uncovered, over medium-high heat, stirring frequently, until juices evaporate.

Add remaining 1 tablespoon butter, melt, and stir in flour; cook, stirring, until bubbly. Add tomatoes, basil, garlic salt, pepper, and sugar. Cook, stirring and breaking up large tomato pieces, until sauce thickens (about 5 minutes).

Blend in 1 tablespoon of the Parmesan cheese. Divide tomato sauce between 2 buttered ramekins (about 1-cup size). Break 1 egg into each. Bake, uncovered, in a 325° oven for 25 minutes for soft-cooked eggs, 30 minutes for firm-cooked. Sprinkle evenly with remaining 2 tablespoons grated Parmesan cheese and chopped parsley.

Scrambled Egg Pizza

Preparation time (cooking included): 15 minutes

Scrambled eggs make a fluffy "crust" for this savory pizza. Add bread sticks and a marinated bean salad to complete a fast skillet dinner for a busy evening.

> 4 eggs
> ¼ cup sour cream
> ¼ teaspoon *each* salt and liquid hot pepper seasoning
> Dash of pepper
> 1½ tablespoons butter or margarine
> ¼ cup *each* shredded Swiss and grated Parmesan cheese
> ½ teaspoon oregano leaves, crumbled
> 3 green onions, thinly sliced
> 4 cherry tomatoes, halved
> 3 thin slices salami, cut in strips
> 2 anchovies (optional)

Beat together eggs, sour cream, salt, hot pepper seasoning, and pepper until blended. Melt butter in small frying pan over medium-low heat. When butter begins to foam, add eggs. Cook, uncovered, lifting cooked portion with a wide spatula to allow uncooked egg to flow under. When eggs are just softly set, remove from heat.

Sprinkle cheeses evenly over eggs; then sprinkle oregano evenly over cheese. Broil about 4 inches from heat just until cheese is melted. Distribute onion over eggs; arrange cherry tomatoes, salami, and anchovies (if used) on top of onion. Cut in wedges.

Individual Omelets

⏱ *Preparation time (cooking included): 10 minutes*

You can turn out individual omelets for one or two people in a very few minutes, once you know how—and it's not difficult to master the technique. You'll need an omelet pan, or any fairly heavy frying pan with sloping sides. For a two or three-egg omelet, a 7 or 8-inch-diameter pan is best. There are endless filling choices; several are given below.

- **2 or 3 eggs**
- **¼ teaspoon salt**
- **Dash of pepper**
- **1 tablespoon water**
- **½ to 1 tablespoon butter or margarine**
- **Filling (optional; suggestions follow)**

For each omelet, break eggs into a small bowl and add salt, pepper, and water. Beat just enough to mix yolks and whites.

Place an omelet pan (or heavy pan with flaring rim and sloping sides) over medium-high heat. To the hot pan add butter and heat until foam begins to subside. Pour in egg mixture all at once. As soon as edges of egg start to turn opaque, slide a spatula under them, lifting so liquid portion runs underneath. Gently shake pan to keep omelet free. Continue to shake pan and lift omelet edges until there is no more liquid but the top still looks moist and creamy.

Sprinkle 2 to 3 tablespoons filling (1 or a combination from suggestions that follow) onto omelet, in line with pan handle. Holding pan in your left hand, slide spatula under right edge of omelet; lift and fold over about ⅓ of omelet. Switch pan to your right hand and tilt over a warm serving plate. Gently shake pan to slide unfolded edge of omelet just onto plate. Flick your right wrist downward so that folded edge of omelet, guided by spatula, falls neatly over omelet edge on plate. Makes 1 serving.

Fillings. Choose 1 or more from this list: shredded **cheese** (jack, Cheddar, or Parmesan); thinly sliced **spinach leaves;** diced **avocado; alfalfa sprouts;** sliced **mushrooms** (raw or sautéed in butter); freshly cooked or canned crumbled **bacon bits;** thinly sliced **ham; salami** slivers; small cooked **shrimp** (or flaked crab or tuna); salted **roasted sunflower seeds;** diced **tomato.**

OPEN-FACED COUNTRY OMELET for two is topped with diced and sautéed potato pieces, crisp bacon, Swiss cheese, parsley, and sautéed walnut halves. Garnish with cream; cut in wedges to serve (recipe at right).

Country Omelet

⏱ *Preparation time (cooking included): 20 minutes*

The toppings for this open-faced omelet are an effective contrast of both flavors and textures: crunchy bacon, bits of cooked potato and onion, chewy cheese, cool sour cream, and crisp sautéed walnuts. (See photograph on facing page.)

- **4 slices bacon**
- **About 8 walnut halves**
- **1 small diced new potato (about ⅛-inch pieces)**
- **¼ cup diced onion**
- **2 tablespoons butter or margarine**
- **3 to 4 eggs, slightly beaten**
- **¼ cup diced (about ⅛-inch pieces) Swiss cheese**
- **2 tablespoons shredded Swiss cheese**
- **1 tablespoon minced parsley**
- **About ¼ cup sour cream**
- **Salt**

In a wide frying pan, cook bacon over medium heat until crisp and browned. Lift out bacon, break into pieces, and set aside. To drippings, add walnuts and cook, stirring, over medium heat 1 to 2 minutes or until lightly browned; set nuts aside. Discard all but 2 tablespoons drippings. Add potatoes and onions and cook, stirring, over medium-low heat until potatoes are soft to bite but only slightly browned (about 10 minutes); remove from pan and set aside; keep warm or reheat.

Clean frying pan to remove any browned particles, then melt butter over medium-low heat. Pour in eggs, pushing them from bottom as they set, allowing uncooked portion to flow down under. When top of omelet is almost set but still a little liquid-looking, sprinkle evenly with potatoes, diced cheese, bacon pieces, shredded cheese, and parsley. Mound sour cream in center of omelet. Garnish with toasted walnuts. Cut into wedges to serve. Salt to taste.

Sausage Scramble

⏱ *Preparation time (cooking included): 15 minutes*

Another good idea for a quick dinner is this interpretation of the classic Western favorite, Joe's Special. Instead of the traditional spinach-ground beef mixture, Italian sausage and Swiss chard team up. Serve it with French bread and butter, and a dry red wine.

- **2 mild Italian sausages (6 to 8 oz. total)**
- **1 small onion, chopped**
- **1 clove garlic, minced or pressed**
- **2 cups finely shredded Swiss chard leaves**
- **3 eggs**
- **Tomato wedges**
- **Grated Parmesan cheese**

(Continued on page 72)

Remove casings from sausages and crumble meat into a small frying pan. Cook, uncovered, over medium-high heat until lightly browned. Add onion and garlic; cook, stirring, until onion is limp. Stir chard leaves into pan (reserve stems for other uses); cook, stirring, until chard is wilted and bright green (about 1 minute). Remove from heat.

Beat eggs until blended; pour over chard mixture and cook over low heat, stirring often, until eggs are just set. Spoon mixture onto warm serving plates. Accompany with tomato wedges and Parmesan cheese to sprinkle over individual servings.

Mexican Scrambled Eggs

Preparation time (cooking included): 15 minutes

Eggs scrambled with mushrooms top crisp cheese-sprinkled tortillas. They are good for brunch or a light supper with a green salad—and for dessert, coconut-strewn orange slices.

- 2 **tablespoons butter or margarine**
- ¼ **pound mushrooms, sliced**
- ¼ **cup sliced green onion**
- 1 **tablespoon seeded and chopped canned California green chiles**
- 2 **flour tortillas**
- 1 **cup (4 oz.) shredded Cheddar or jack cheese**
- 4 **eggs**
- ¼ **teaspoon salt**
- 1 **small avocado, peeled, pitted, and sliced Red or green taco sauce**

Melt butter in a frying pan over medium heat. Add mushrooms, onion, and chiles; cook, uncovered, until mushrooms are limp and liquid has evaporated (about 5 minutes).

Meanwhile, arrange tortillas on a baking sheet; sprinkle evenly with cheese and place in a 350° oven until cheese is melted (about 4 minutes). Beat eggs and salt until blended; pour into mushroom mixture and cook, lifting cooked portion with a wide spatula to allow uncooked egg to flow under. Cook until done to your liking. Spoon eggs over cheese-topped tortillas; top with avocado slices. Pass taco sauce. Serve with knife and fork.

Florentine Spinach with Eggs

Preparation time: 20 minutes. Cooking time: 8 minutes

Egg yolks bake in a hollow of puffy egg white topping an individual serving of spinach and cheese. Serve this quickly made entrée for brunch, lunch, or a late supper.

- 1 **package (10 oz.) frozen chopped spinach, thawed**
  Dash of nutmeg
- 2 **tablespoons sour cream**
- ¼ **teaspoon prepared mustard**
- 4 **green onions, thinly sliced**
- 2 **slices (2 oz. total) jack cheese**
- 4 **eggs, separated**
- ½ **teaspoon cream of tartar**
- ¼ **teaspoon salt**

Put spinach into a wire strainer and press out liquid. Mix spinach, nutmeg, sour cream, and mustard. Divide between 2 greased 1¼ cup individual casseroles or soufflé dishes. Reserve half the onion; evenly distribute remaining onion over spinach mixture. Top each casserole with a slice of cheese. Bake in a 475° oven for 4 to 5 minutes or until heated through.

In a bowl beat egg whites, cream of tartar, and salt until eggs form stiff, distinct peaks.

Remove casseroles from oven and immediately cover with egg white topping. With spoon, make a ½-inch-deep depression in center of each and slip 2 egg yolks into each. Return to oven; continue to bake for 4 to 6 minutes, until topping begins to brown. Sprinkle remaining onion over tops.

Egg Enchiladas

Preparation time: 15 minutes. Cooking time: 13 minutes

For a quick enchilada filling, try eggs scrambled with green chiles. This dish makes a good meatless supper when you add an iceberg lettuce salad and warm refried beans topped with thinly sliced green onion.

1½ tablespoons salad oil
 1 small onion, chopped
 ½ cup chopped green pepper
 1 large can (15 oz.) tomato sauce
1½ teaspoons chili powder
 5 eggs
 2 tablespoons half-and-half (light cream) or milk
1½ tablespoons seeded, chopped canned California green chiles
   Salt and pepper
1½ tablespoons butter or margarine
 4 corn tortillas
 ¾ cup shredded Cheddar cheese

Heat oil in a frying pan over medium heat. Add onion and green pepper and cook, uncovered, until limp. Add tomato sauce and chili powder; simmer, uncovered, for about 10 minutes.

Beat eggs lightly with half-and-half; add chiles, and salt and pepper to taste.

Melt butter in frying pan over medium-low heat; add eggs and cook until softly set; keep warm.

Dip each tortilla in hot tomato sauce until soft; spoon ¼ of the scrambled eggs down center. Turn part of tortilla over filling, roll, and place seam side down in a shallow baking dish. Reheat remaining sauce to boiling, pour over top, and sprinkle with cheese. Place under broiler 4 inches from heat until cheese melts (about 3 minutes). Makes 2 servings of 2 enchiladas each.

Show-stopper Dutch Baby Pancake

Made with eggy batter like that used for popovers, this pancake puffs up dramatically in the oven. The results are especially spectacular when the batter is baked in a big container such as a paella pan. Whatever the shape of the pan, it should be fairly shallow—not much over 3 inches deep. Pick your pan; measure its total volume by pouring in quart measures of water.

Serve the pancake for breakfast, lunch, or supper. It's delicious with fruit topping either spooned over or served alongside.

For a 2 to 3-quart pan, use ¼ cup **butter** or margarine, 3 **eggs,** and ¾ cup *each* **milk** and **all-purpose flour.**

For a 3 to 4-quart pan, use ⅓ cup **butter** or margarine, 4 **eggs,** and 1 cup *each* **milk** and **all-purpose flour.**

Place butter in pan and set in a 425° oven. While butter melts, mix batter quickly.

Put eggs in a blender or food processor and whirl at high speed for 1 minute. With motor running, gradually pour in milk, then slowly add flour; continue whirling for 30 seconds.

Remove pan from oven, pour in batter, and bake until puffy and well browned (20 to 25 minutes, depending on pan size).

Dust pancake with **ground nutmeg,** if you wish, and serve at once with any of the following **toppings. Makes 2 servings.**

Pancake Toppings

Fresh fruit. Serve a bowl of sliced strawberries, sweetened to taste; or defrosted frozen peach slices; or any fruits in season, cut and sweetened.

Hot fruit. Sauté fresh apple or pear slices in a little butter or margarine until tender and translucent. Sweeten with sugar or honey to taste and offer with cinnamon-sugar and sour cream or yogurt. Or heat banana or papaya slices in melted butter or margarine over medium heat, turning, until hot; serve with lime wedges.

Canned pie filling. To cherry or apple pie filling, add lemon juice and ground cinnamon to taste. Serve cold or warmed, topped with yogurt or sour cream.

Powdered sugar. Have a shaker or bowl of powdered sugar and thick wedges of lemon at the table. Sprinkle sugar on hot pancake, then squeeze lemon over.

Syrups. Pass warm honey, maple syrup, or any favorite fruit syrup.

Cheese, Onion, and Chile Pie

🕐 *Preparation time: 20 minutes. Cooking time: 38 minutes*

Here is a cheese pie with a Mexican accent—sour cream, green chiles, and two mild cheeses. A good companion is a crisp green salad with cherry tomatoes and sliced avocado.

Buttery pastry shell (see crab quiche recipe, this page)
2 tablespoons butter or margarine
1 large onion, thinly sliced
1 cup sour cream
2 eggs
Dash of salt
¼ cup seeded and chopped canned California green chiles
⅔ cup *each* shredded jack and Longhorn Cheddar cheese

Prepare pastry shell. Melt butter in a small frying pan over medium heat. Add onion and cook, stirring, until limp and slightly browned (8 to 10 minutes); remove from heat and cool slightly.

Meanwhile, beat together sour cream, eggs, and salt; stir in chiles, cooled onion mixture, jack cheese, and ⅓ cup of the Cheddar. Spread filling in cooled pastry shell and bake in a 350° oven until filling is almost set (about 25 minutes). Sprinkle with remaining ⅓ cup Cheddar cheese, return to oven, and continue baking for 5 minutes longer or until custard is set when pan is jiggled. Let stand for a few minutes to cool slightly before cutting in wedges to serve.

Crab Quiche

🕐 *Preparation time: 20 minutes. Cooking time: 1 hour*

For brunch or a late evening supper, serve this crab quiche, elegant in its buttery pastry crust. Complement it with a well-chilled champagne or dry white wine. (See photograph on facing page.)

Buttery pastry shell (recipe follows)
½ cup shredded Swiss, Samsoe, or Gruyère cheese
6 ounces (about 1½ cups) cooked or canned crab meat, flaked
¼ cup finely chopped onion
1 tablespoon dry sherry (optional)
1 tablespoon finely chopped parsley
Dash of cayenne pepper
⅛ teaspoon tarragon, crumbled
2 eggs
1 cup half-and-half (light cream)
Paprika

Prepare pastry shell. When cool, evenly sprinkle cheese over bottom of shell. Combine crab, onion, sherry, parsley, cayenne, and tarragon; spoon over cheese. Beat eggs with cream and pour over crab. Sprinkle lightly with paprika. Bake in a 325° oven for 45 to 50 minutes or until custard appears firm when dish is gently shaken. Let stand for a few minutes to cool slightly before cutting in wedges to serve.

Buttery pastry shell. In a bowl, cut 3 tablespoons firm butter or margarine into ¾ cup unsifted all-purpose flour until mixture forms coarse crumbs. With a fork, lightly stir in 1 egg yolk. Add 3 to 4 teaspoons cold water, a little at a time, stirring until pastry clings together. Use your hands to form it into a ball.

Roll pastry out on a floured board or pastry cloth into a circle about 2 inches larger in diameter than an 8-inch quiche or pie pan. Fit pastry into pan; trim edge. Pierce bottom and sides all over with a fork. Bake in a 400° oven for 8 to 10 minutes or until pastry begins to brown. Let cool on a rack.

Cheese Ramekins

🕐 *Preparation time: 10 minutes. Chilling time: 2 hours. Cooking time: 20 minutes*

This make-ahead brunch dish bears some resemblance to both a cheese fondue and a quiche. A white wine cheese custard saturates the buttered bread base and puffs it up when baked. Serve with link sausage and fruit.

Butter or margarine, at room temperature
2 slices white bread
2 eggs
1 cup half-and-half (light cream) or milk
¼ cup dry white wine
⅛ teaspoon *each* salt and dry mustard
1½ cups shredded Swiss cheese
2 thinly sliced green onions

Spread butter on both sides of bread; place in shallow individual baking dishes (about 1-cup size). Beat eggs until light, then beat in half-and-half, wine, salt, and mustard. Evenly distribute cheese over bread, then pour egg mixture over, dividing evenly. Sprinkle onion slices over top. Cover and chill for at least 2 hours or until next day.

Bake, uncovered, in a 350° oven for 20 to 25 minutes or until custard appears set when jiggled.

AN INTIMATE GARDEN PARTY features golden crab quiche, served hot or cold (recipe at left), and avocado halves filled with Russian dressing. Let the champagne flow.

And in Conclusion...Desserts

Whether dessert for the two of you is an almost-always routine or an almost-never treat, you'll be intrigued by the possibilities for making special sweets on a small scale. Here we present ideas for lifting ice cream, puddings, and fruit from the mundane to the marvelous. And then there are the miniatures—little individual tarts, soufflés, even a cheesecake, sized to satisfy, not to overwhelm.

Meringue Heart Sundaes

For Valentine's day or any other romantic occasion, fill heart-shaped meringue shells with ice cream and top with a crimson fruit sauce.

With an electric mixer, beat 1 **egg white** and ⅛ teaspoon **cream of tartar** until very foamy. Gradually sprinkle in ¼ cup **sugar**, 1 tablespoon at a time, beating well after each addition. Beat until meringue holds very stiff peaks. Add ¼ teaspoon **vanilla**; beat for about 30 seconds longer.

Cover a baking sheet with baking parchment or brown wrapping paper. Draw 2 heart shapes, each 5 inches across at the widest point, on the paper. With a spatula or knife, spread meringue over heart shape, building up sides so they stand ½ to ¾ inch high.

Bake in a 275° oven for 45 minutes; then turn oven off and let meringue shells dry in oven for 1½ hours. Wrap each airtight if made ahead.

To serve, thaw 1 cup **unsweetened frozen strawberries** (crush a few to make some juice), then sweeten berries and juice to taste with **sugar.** (You can substitute strawberry-flavored ice cream topping.) Fill each meringue heart with a large scoop of **strawberry ice cream;** top with berry sauce.

Peppermint Tapioca Parfaits

Layer the minty pudding with chocolate cooky crumbs in parfait glasses for this pretty make-ahead dessert. (See photograph on page 78.)

In a pan, mix 1½ tablespoons *each* **quick-cooking tapioca** and **sugar,** 1 cup **milk,** dash **salt,** and 1 **egg yolk;** let stand for 5 minutes. Beat 1 **egg white** until very foamy; then gradually sprinkle in 1 tablespoon **sugar,** beating until soft peaks form; set aside.

Cook tapioca mixture over medium heat, stirring constantly, until it comes to a full boil (about 6 to 8 minutes). Remove from heat and gently fold in beaten egg white just until blended. Stir in ½ teaspoon **vanilla** and a few drops **red food coloring,** if desired. Let cool, uncovered, for 30 minutes. Fold in 3 tablespoons crushed **peppermint candy.** Cover and chill. Meanwhile, crush enough **chocolate cookies** to make ⅓ cup crumbs.

To serve, place about 1 tablespoon crumbs in each of 2 parfait glasses (at least 1-cup size). Top with several spoonfuls tapioca mixture; repeat layers, ending with a sprinkling of crumbs. Cover and chill if made ahead. Garnish with mint sprigs, if desired.

One-Apple Pie

One good-sized apple, sliced and mixed with sugar and spice, makes one nice-sized apple pie for two.

First make pastry: In a bowl combine ⅓ cup **all-purpose flour** (unsifted), 1 teaspoon **sugar,** and 2 tablespoons **butter** or margarine; rub with fingers until evenly mixed. With a fork stir in 1 tablespoon **milk** until dough holds together. Press into a ball and cut in half. Roll out one portion on a floured board until large enough to fit a 4 to 5-inch pie pan. With some pastry extending beyond rim, fit pastry into pan.

Peel, core, and slice 1 medium-size Golden Delicious or Newton Pippin apple. Mix with 1 to 2 tablespoons sugar and ¼ teaspoon ground cinnamon. Pile fruit into pastry-lined pan. Roll out remaining pastry on floured board until large enough to cover apples. Fold pastry edges together to seal in fruit, then crimp rim. Prick top and sprinkle lightly with sugar.

Bake pie on lowest rack in a 375° oven for about 45 minutes or until crust is well browned. Let cool; serve slightly warm or cold.

Caramel Custard

Caramelized sugar coats the bottoms of the cups in which the custard bakes, creating a sauce.

In a small frying pan over medium heat, melt 2½ tablespoons **sugar,** shaking pan as sugar begins to liquefy and caramelize. When liquid (do not let scorch), pour at once, equally, into 2 small, deep individual baking dishes (*each* at least ¾-cup size).

In a bowl, beat until blended, but not frothy, 2 **eggs,** 2 tablespoons **sugar,** and ¼ teaspoon **vanilla.** Bring 1 cup **milk** to scalding and stir into eggs. Pour an equal portion into each baking dish.

Set dishes in a rimmed pan and place in a 350° oven; at once pour **boiling water** into pan to a depth of about 1 inch.

Bake for about 30 minutes or until center of custard jiggles only slightly when a dish is shaken gently. Lift from water at once and let cool. Serve at room temperature; or cover and chill for as long as 2 days.

Run a knife between custard and dish, then invert onto individual serving plates.

Fresh Raspberry Tarts

A tender press-in pastry enhances a filling of fresh berries. Bake the tart shells ahead and freeze them, if you like. (See photograph on page 18.)

From a total of 1½ cups **raspberries,** measure ½ cup and put in a blender or food processor. Add ¼ cup **sugar** and 2 tablespoons **water;** whirl until smooth. (If you wish, pour through a wire strainer and discard seeds.)

In a pan, blend puréed berries with 1 tablespoon **cornstarch.** Cook over medium-high heat, stirring constantly, until thickened and clear. Remove from heat and stir in ½ teaspoon **lemon juice** and a dash **ground nutmeg.** Gently mix in remaining 1 cup berries. Evenly spoon berry filling into **tart shells** (recipe follows) and serve hot, warm, or chilled. Top each tart with **whipped cream** or ice cream, if you like. Makes 2 tarts.

Tart shells. Mix ½ cup **all-purpose flour** (unsifted), 1 tablespoon **powdered sugar,** and a dash **salt.** With 2 knives cut in 3 tablespoons firm **butter** or margarine until mixture is uniformly crumbly. Stir 1 **egg yolk** into flour mixture, then use your hands to press dough together; divide into 2 equal parts. Press pastry evenly into 2 pie pans, each 4½ inches in diameter. Pierce bottom and sides all over with a fork. Bake in a 325° oven for 18 to 20 minutes or until golden brown. Cool in pans on a rack. Leave in tins or carefully remove shells to fill.

Individual Soufflés with Cherry Sauce

These fluffy little soufflés bake while you're eating the main course. Enjoy them hot from the oven, with a steaming cherry sauce poured over.

Butter 2 individual soufflé dishes (1-cup size) and sprinkle lightly with **sugar.** Beat 1 **egg white** until very foamy. Gradually sprinkle in 1½ tablespoons **sugar,** beating until stiff peaks form. In another bowl, stir together 1 **egg yolk,** ½ cup **sour cream,** 1½ tablespoons **sugar,** ½ teaspoon **grated lemon peel,** and a dash of **salt.** Fold into beaten egg white. Spoon mixture equally into soufflé dishes.

Bake in a 350° oven for 20 minutes or until soufflés jiggle only slightly when dishes are gently shaken; serve at once. Pass hot **cherry sauce** (recipe follows) to spoon over each.

Cherry sauce. Drain 1 small can (9 oz.) **pitted dark sweet cherries,** reserving syrup. In a pan, combine syrup, 1 tablespoon **sugar,** and 1½ teaspoons **cornstarch.** Cook, stirring, over medium-high heat, until sauce boils and thickens. Remove from heat, stir in cherries and ¼ teaspoon **brandy** or rum flavoring. Serve hot.

Cream Cheesecake

A 3-ounce cheesecake, split two ways, is everything your sweet tooth requires. Working with small quantities, you press in and bake a crust, then fill it with a cream cheese mixture.

In a small bowl, combine 3 tablespoons **all-purpose flour,** 1 tablespoon **sugar,** and 1 tablespoon **butter** or margarine. Rub between your fingers until evenly mixed. Turn into a greased 4½ to 5-inch-diameter round container and press firmly in bottom. Bake in a 325° oven for 15 to 20 minutes or until crust is lightly browned. Remove from oven.

While crust bakes, mash 1 small package (3 oz.) **cream cheese** (at room temperature) with a fork. Blend in 1 tablespoon **sugar,** ⅛ teaspoon grated **lemon peel,** ¼ teaspoon **vanilla,** and 1 **egg,** mixing well. Pour into baked crust. Bake in a 325° oven for 15 minutes or until filling appears set when pan is gently jiggled.

Meanwhile, mix 2 tablespoons **sour cream** and 1 teaspoon **sugar.** When you take cheesecake from oven, at once spread with sour cream mixture. Chill, then serve.